Calphalon Cooks Weeknights

By the Culinary Staff at Calphalon

Calphalon®

Sunset
BOOKS

Developmental Editor
   Linda J. Selden

Art Directors
   Vasken Guiragossian and
   Pamela Hoch

Design
   Tyrone James Drake

Research & Text
   Sandra Cameron and
   Cynthia Scheer

Copy Editor
   Rebecca LaBrum

Photography
   Chris Shorten

Food Stylist
   Susan Massey

Food Stylist Assistant
   Kim Konecny

Prop Stylist
   Laura Ferguson

Sunset Books

President & Publisher
   Susan J. Maruyama

Editorial Director
   Bob Doyle

A Word About Our Nutritional Data

For our recipes, we provide a nutritional analysis stating calorie count; grams of total fat and saturated fat; milligrams of cholesterol and sodium; grams of carbohydrates, fiber, and protein; and milligrams of calcium and iron. Generally, the analysis applies to a single serving, based on the number of servings given for each recipe and the amount of each ingredient. If a range is given for the number of servings and/or the amount of an ingredient, the analysis is based on the average of the figures given.

The nutritional analysis does not include optional ingredients or those for which no specific amount is stated. If an ingredient is listed with substitution, the information was calculated using the first choice.

Preparation and cooking times are provided for each recipe. Keep in mind that these times are approximate and will vary depending on your expertise in the kitchen and on the cooking equipment you use.

CONTENTS

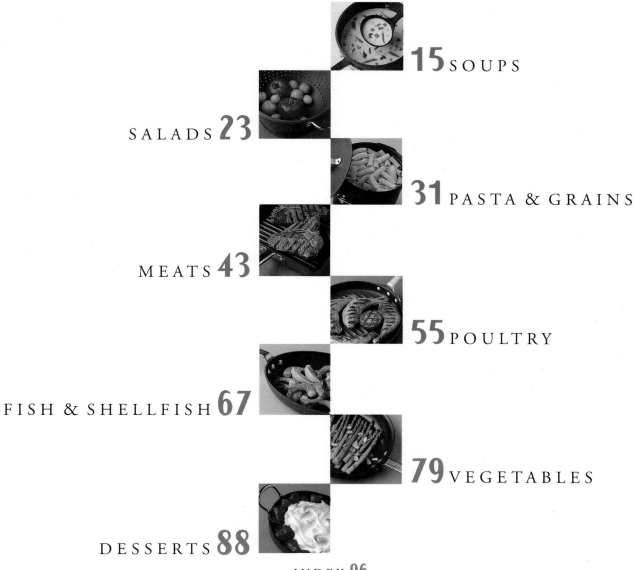

Meals for Busy Weeknights

For interesting and delicious dishes that fit your busy weekday schedule, turn to Calphalon cookware and this book. You'll find ideas for soups, salads, main dishes, vegetable specialties, even desserts—and almost all can be prepared in under an hour. Use the preparation and cooking times that accompany each recipe as a general guide; choose a speedier dish such as Black Bean Soup (page 20) when you're really rushed, a longer-cooking one like Belgian Beer Stew (page 47) when you have more time. Each recipe also includes serving suggestions to give you ideas for putting together a complete menu.

COOKING WITH CALPHALON

Quality and versatility are two good reasons to choose durable *Calphalon Hard-Anodized Cookware* for preparing weeknight meals. The handsome pans are made from heavy-gauge aluminum, one of the most conductive of all metals used for cookware.

First spun or drawn into one of many classic shapes and sizes, the pans then undergo the electrochemical process of hard-anodization—giving them a hard, non-porous surface that's an integral part of each pan, not just a surface coating. That means you can use a metal spatula or tongs for turning foods and a wire whisk to stir sauces when you cook in Calphalon. These pans are matchless for a wide variety of cooking techniques, from preparing a classic omelette to sautéing shrimp, chicken, or crisp vegetables.

When minutes count, you can depend on Calphalon pans to heat quickly and evenly. Because heat is distributed so uniformly over the pans' smooth surface, food seldom sticks during cooking. What's more, meats, poultry, and fish brown beautifully in a Calphalon omelette pan or sauté pan, enabling you to finish off a quick sautéed dish such as Fillet of Sole with Shallots, Vermouth & Thyme (page 68) with a stylish sauce that takes advantage of the flavorful pan drippings.

Some styles of Calphalon pans have long handles of sturdy nickel-chrome plated cast iron, while others have loop handles of nickel-chrome plated steel. Such pans are appropriate for cooking on the range top as well as for baking or broiling—versatility that can save you time when you start a dish (such as Baked Halibut Provençal, page 72) on top of the range, then complete it in the oven.

CARING FOR YOUR CALPHALON

The most important step in keeping Calphalon cookware in top-notch condition is washing it thoroughly (by hand, *not* in the dishwasher) in hot, sudsy water after each use. If any cooking residue remains, use a Scotch-Brite® pad to remove it, with a household cleanser such as Ajax® or Comet® if necessary. Dormond, a cleanser made specifically for Calphalon, can also be used; look for it in stores where Calphalon is sold.

Keep your Calphalon cookware in shape by taking care not to hit the rim with the sharp handle of a spoon or other utensil as you cook. And do your cutting and chopping before you place food in the pan; using a sharp knife in the pan itself can mar the surface.

After you finish cooking, let the pan cool completely; then, if necessary, pour water into it to loosen cooked-on food. Never immerse a warm pan in cold water, since it may become warped.

Many Calphalon pans—the oval au gratin pan and the paella pan in particular—are so handsome that they can go directly from the kitchen to the table. After the meal is over, promptly transfer any leftovers to another container, so the food can be cooled quickly and then covered airtight for storage in the refrigerator.

OTHER KINDS
OF CALPHALON COOKWARE

Calphalon makes more than one kind of cookware. *Professional Nonstick from Calphalon*, made with the same materials and in the same way as Calphalon Hard-Anodized Cookware, is especially useful for low-fat cooking. Professional Nonstick pans are coated inside and out with nonstick material and can be wiped clean with a sponge. Their covers are made of tempered glass with stainless steel rims. Both pans and lids can be used in the oven up to a temperature of 450°F, but they should not go under the broiler.

Handwashing is recommended for Professional Nonstick pans; also be sure to give them a hot, sudsy bath before you first use them. During cooking, use nylon, plastic, or wooden spoons and spatulas to preserve the nonstick surface.

Bon Ami® or Soft Scrub® and a soft plastic sponge can be used to remove any stains on the outsides of this cookware.

For those who prefer to cook in stainless steel, there's *Professional Tri-Ply Stainless from Calphalon*. This cookware has an inner core of aluminum surrounded by two layers of stainless steel. The bottom surfaces are brushed for durability, the pan sides are polished, the interiors are satin-finished, and the pan rims are slightly flared to make pouring easy. Pan lids are made of tempered glass. These pans are oven and broiler safe, but the lids should not be used under the broiler or in an oven hotter than 450°F.

Professional Stainless can be washed in the dishwasher, but you'll keep it spot-free and shinier if you wash it by hand. To remove any stuck-on food, nonabrasive cleansers such as Bon Ami, Soft Scrub, and Bar Keepers Friend® are recommended.

For home baking, there's now sturdy *Professional Nonstick Bakeware from Calphalon*: standard-size cookie sheets, loaf pans, muffin pans, and round, square, and rectangular cake pans. All are made from heavy-gauge aluminum or aluminized steel, following the construction techniques used for commercial bakeware.

Professional Nonstick Bakeware has a triple-coated nonstick finish inside and a medium-gray color coating outside, allowing it to absorb and reflect heat well for good texture and browning—for everything from a batch of corn muffins to a one-pan dessert like Quick Chocolate Cake (page 95). To cut and remove food from these pans, use a coated or nylon spatula, since repeated use of metal utensils will damage the surface.

Like any cookware, Professional Nonstick Bakeware should be washed in hot, sudsy water before the first use. After using a pan, remove any food residue with a sponge or soft cloth and hot, sudsy water. Baked-on stains on a pan's exterior can be removed with Bon Ami or Soft Scrub and a soft nylon cleaning pad.

Basic Kitchen Equipment for Weeknight Cooking

If your kitchen includes these fundamental pieces of cookware, you'll be able to create delicious weeknight meals with speed and skill.

COOKWARE

8-, 10-, or 12-inch omelette pan: With wide bottoms and gently sloping sides, these are practical not only for omelettes and frittatas, but also for sautéing mushrooms and other vegetables and for quickly cooking steaks, chops, chicken breasts, and fish fillets.

2-, 3-, or 5-quart sauté pan: In addition to sautéing, these versatile straight-sided, flat-bottomed, covered pans can also be used for braising and deep-frying, and as covered casseroles.

2- and 4-quart sauce pans: You'll use these basic pans for everything from boiling water to cooking rice for Risotto with Mushrooms & Asparagus (page 39) to whisking a creamy cheese sauce. The covered pans absorb and hold heat well for slow, even cooking, and their rounded edges make it easy to stir sauces smoothly. Add a **vegetable steamer insert** for even more versatility.

8-quart stock pot: Tall and narrow, this pan is for cooking stock or soup at a leisurely simmer—or for bringing water for pasta to a furious boil. To drain pasta, you might want to add the corresponding **pasta insert.**

5-quart saucier: A deep, covered pan of this sort is ideal for long, slow cooking on top of the range or in the oven. It's also handy for a family-size main-dish soup or chili.

Large roasting pan with rack: This capacious low, open pan easily holds a roast or chicken surrounded with vegetables. Once the food has baked to savory perfection, remove it from the pan. Spoon the fat from the pan drippings; then deglaze the pan with broth or wine to make a complementary sauce, following the manufacturer's instructions for your particular roasting pan.

PANS FOR BAKING

Medium or large cookie sheets (2): When you make cookies, biscuits and scones, pizza, or free-form loaves of bread, you'll find they bake and brown evenly when you use heavy-gauge nonstick baking sheets.

8- or 9-inch-round cake pans (2 or 3): Whether you're baking from a package mix or using a treasured family recipe, your cakes will rise and brown evenly in these professional-quality layer pans.

8-inch-square pan: Here's the classic pan for a speedy cornbread to set off Black Bean Soup (page 20) or for warm, fudgy brownies to top with ice cream for an impromptu dessert.

9- by 13-inch pan: In a pinch, you can bake or (with the addition of a rack) roast almost anything in this all-purpose rectangular baking pan. It's perfect when you need a cake to take to a picnic or potluck.

4½- by 8½-inch or 5- by 10-inch loaf pans (2): You'll need these for quick fruit and nut breads, yeast breads, and for that all-time weeknight favorite, meat loaf.

12-cup muffin pan: Muffins are the quickest of all breads, and they brown and rise beautifully in this handsome pan. The muffin pan can also be used for cupcakes and classic yeast dinner rolls.

OTHER KITCHEN ESSENTIALS

Without this basic equipment, it's not easy to achieve the efficiency needed to put dinner together fast. Be sure your kitchen includes these:

Colander: Use for rinsing and draining fruits and vegetables, salad greens, and pasta.

Cutlery: Your knife rack should include a **chef's knife** (also known as a French knife) for chopping and mincing vegetables; a **paring knife** for peeling, seeding, and pitting; a **slicing knife** for thinly slicing large cuts of meat; a serrated **bread knife**; and a **sharpening steel** to keep knife edges keen.

Good-size cutting board: Scrub it with hot, soapy water after each use to prevent food-borne contamination.

Mixing bowls: It's preferable to have a nested set ranging from tiny to immense. Tempered glass is useful when you use the bowls for hot liquids.

Wire strainer: This can pinch-hit for a flour sifter; it can also be used to drain pasta or grains that are too small for your colander.

Cooling racks: These protect your counters and let hot baked foods cool evenly.

MEASURING EQUIPMENT

Measuring cups: Include a set of **dry** measuring cups (in ¼-, ⅓-, ½-, and 1-cup sizes) for leveling off dry ingredients, as well as a set of **liquid** measuring cups (in 1-, 2-, and 4-cup sizes) with pouring spouts.

Measuring spoons: A standard set includes ¼-teaspoon, ½-teaspoon, 1-teaspoon, and 1-tablespoon measures. Use for both liquid and dry ingredients.

Kitchen scale: While not essential, it takes the guesswork out of determining weights of produce, pasta, and meat, poultry, or seafood when you're not sure how much you have on hand.

UTENSILS

Don't dismiss them as mere gadgets! The items on this list can make the difference between success and failure—and save precious minutes—in many a dish.

- Mixing spoons (nylon, coated, or wooden if your cookware has nonstick surfaces)
- Slotted spoon
- Vegetable peeler (for potatoes, carrots, apples, etc.)
- Whisks (for making lump-free sauces)
- Spatulas (metal, nylon, and rubber)
- Tongs (for lifting and turning)
- Zester (for removing citrus zest for flavoring and garnishes)
- Timer (even if you use the one on your oven, it's convenient to have a second, portable model)
- Citrus juicer (for squeezing juice from lemons, oranges, limes, and grapefruit)
- Instant-read thermometer (for determining the precise internal temperature of meat, poultry, or fish)
- Grater (for shredded or grated cheese, chocolate, carrots, etc.)
- Can opener (manual or electric)
- Rolling pin (for shaping pastry and biscuits, both homemade and from refrigerated or frozen doughs)
- Wine opener
- Garlic press
- Brushes (for applying bastes and marinades to meats and poultry and for brushing pastries with beaten egg or egg whites)
- Pepper mill (filled with whole black peppercorns or with a mixture of peppercorns in different colors)

SMALL APPLIANCES

Real time savings are possible when you make the most of these multipurpose kitchen helpers.

- Electric mixer (if you bake a lot, both a heavy-duty mixer and a portable one)
- Blender
- Food processor
- Toaster oven

KITCHEN SAFETY

For protection from accidental cooking fires, be sure your kitchen is equipped with a **fire extinguisher** and that the adjacent area contains a properly installed **smoke detector.**

Kitchen Equipment

A roasting pan with rack
B 3-quart sauté pan
C cutting board
D bread knife
E casserole
F pepper mill
G dry measuring cups
H chef's knife
I sharpening steel
J 10-inch omelette pan
K 4-quart sauce pan
L 2-quart sauce pan
M 8-quart stock pot
N colander
O cooking utensils
P grater
Q electric mixer
R rolling pin
S cookie sheets
T round cake pans
U muffin pan
V 8-inch-square pan
W loaf pans
X 9- by 13-inch pan
Y 12-inch omelette pan
Z steamer insert

Basic Cooking Techniques

Take time to learn a few new techniques when you cook with your Calphalon cookware. The reward will be time saved as you cook the best weeknight meals you and your family have ever tasted! For every kind of cooking, remember that the first important step is to start with a clean pan.

SAUTÉING

As you assemble ingredients and utensils for a meal, remove refrigerated foods first. That way the food will be a bit less cold and can start cooking as soon as you place it in the pan.

Preheat the pan before you begin to sauté food. This enables the pan—and the oil or butter you'll add next—to be at the right temperature for browning (or searing) the surface of meat or other food as soon as you add it to the pan. Preheating also minimizes sticking.

When preheating, use this "hot-to-the-touch" test. Place the pan over medium to medium-high heat. When it is properly preheated, the rim will feel hot when you touch it lightly. Test by adding a small piece of butter to the pan. If the butter bubbles briskly but does not burn, the pan is preheated to the right temperature. Add the butter or oil specified in the recipe, then heat for about 1 more minute before adding the food.

Follow the recipe as you continue cooking, using the heat setting called for in each recipe (this will vary depending on the type and quantity of food). Remember that Calphalon cookware is so conductive that heat travels quickly throughout the pan, often allowing you to maintain the perfect temperature at a lower heat setting than you might expect. Experiment until you find the right one. When you sauté, use a pan large enough to cook all the pieces of food without crowding them. If there's too much food in the pan, liquid will collect and the food will steam in it. When you sauté, you want as little moisture as possible in the pan.

To turn food, use a flexible metal or plastic spatula with a thin edge that slips easily under the browned surface of each piece.

DEGLAZING

After you sauté meat, poultry, or fish and remove it from the pan, the pan will be glazed with drippings that can be the beginning of a quick and easy sauce. Over medium-high heat, pour in a flavorful liquid such as broth, red or white wine or vermouth, or fruit juice. Stir with a spoon or spatula until all the drippings are mixed with the liquid and the sauce is reduced to an almost syrupy consistency. Pork Tenderloin with Stilton & Port (page 51) is topped with a creamy sauce made by this technique.

STIR-FRYING

The superior conductivity of Calphalon cookware makes it a natural for stir-frying. Take a look at the recipe for Coconut Basil Chicken (page 59) to see how all the elements are cooked and stirred over high or medium-high heat so that all surfaces of the food make maximum contact with the pan's hot surface.

A stir-fry pan or wok is ideal for recipes of this type, but you can also use an omelette pan or sauté pan. To prepare the pan for stir-frying, preheat it over high or medium-high heat. When the pan rim is hot-to-the-touch, add the amount of oil the recipe specifies and heat for about 1 more minute. Then proceed as the recipe directs. If you need additional oil to cook subsequent ingredients, be sure to heat it briefly before continuing with stir-frying.

Simple Sauce-making

With Calphalon cookware, sauces are close to foolproof. You can make them confidently, with no worries about lumps or spots that cling to the pan. Here are a few simple guidelines.

For a flour- or cornstarch-thickened sauce, heat the pan over medium heat until the rim is hot-to-the-touch (see "Sautéing," facing page). Add a bit of the butter specified in the recipe and heat until it begins to bubble; add remaining butter, swirling the pan over the heat until the butter is melted. Using a whisk, blend in the flour and cook, stirring constantly, until bubbly. Remove the pan from the heat and gradually stir in the milk or other liquid in the recipe. Return the pan to the heat and continue to cook, stirring, until the sauce boils and thickens.

When you make an egg-thickened sauce, use low heat for cooking; whisk or stir until the sauce has thickened as called for in the recipe. Keep the heat low and stir the sauce constantly. Be sure your spoon or whisk is small enough to reach every part of the pan.

The hard-anodized surface of Calphalon cookware will not interact with ingredients in either of these kinds of sauces to cause discoloration. And the pans conduct heat so perfectly that delicate sauces cook gently, with little chance of separating or curdling.

Range-top Grilling

You can use a Calphalon rectangular, round, or square griddle or one of the shallow, flat-bottomed omelette or sauté pans for foods such as pancakes and grilled sandwiches. And to give steak, lamb chops, or sausages an authentically grilled look when it's not convenient to grill outdoors, choose a Calphalon grill pan. The ridges allow fat to drain away from the meat—and they produce handsome grill marks, too.

Preheat the pan over medium to medium-high heat. Test the heat by rubbing the pan with a bit of butter; it should bubble but not burn. Add a little more butter or oil as needed for the food you plan to grill; then let the pan heat briefly. Add foods and cook until the underside is golden; then turn with a flexible metal spatula and brown on the other side.

If you're cooking in batches, clean the pan as needed between batches by sprinkling it with salt, then rubbing it with a paper towel moistened with oil.

Foods Cooked in Liquid

When you cook food in a quantity of water—that is, when you make broth or stock, boil or steam potatoes or other vegetables, or cook pasta—it isn't necessary to preheat your Calphalon cookware. Just place the liquid in the pan and proceed as directed in your recipe. You can use high heat to maintain a rapid boil.

To make a meaty broth or stock, start the mixture over medium-high heat so that it comes to a boil gradually; then reduce the heat to medium-low and let the stock cook at a simmer—hot enough for the liquid to tremble with no bubbles breaking the surface.

A Calphalon pasta insert is useful for draining cooked pasta. When you make broth, you can also use the insert to lift out the bones and vegetables after the stock is done.

Baking in Calphalon

Prepare Professional Nonstick Bakeware following recipe instructions, greasing and flouring pans (or lining muffin pans with paper baking cups) if the recipe directs you to do so. Be sure to preheat your oven to the specified temperature.

Browning may be faster in Professional Nonstick Bakeware, so begin checking for doneness a little in advance of the specified time. As you try your favorite recipes in this bakeware, you may find you can adjust oven temperatures and baking times downward. Use these pans for baking only; they should not be used for broiling.

A Well-stocked Pantry

Always keep your kitchen well stocked: It's less trouble to produce a satisfying meal when you can depend on a good supply of the staple foods you cook with often. Here are some of the items that a resourceful pantry should contain. Of course, your list may differ depending on your family's food preferences.

Be sure to keep track of your supplies so you can replenish them as needed when you shop for perishable foods.

Many of the recipes in this book call for nonfat, low-fat, and reduced-sodium varieties of these items, and they're worth seeking out when you shop.

ON THE PANTRY SHELF

Many of these foods should be refrigerated after opening.

- Canned tomatoes (diced, pear-shaped, seasoned stewed)
- Tomato sauce
- Tomato paste
- Sun-dried tomatoes
- Tuna
- Anchovy fillets
- Marinated artichoke hearts
- Canned beans (black; red and/or white kidney)
- Olives (whole and sliced ripe, calamata, Niçoise, pimento-stuffed green)
- Mango chutney
- Honey
- Peanut butter
- Soy sauce
- Worcestershire sauce
- Liquid hot pepper seasoning
- Canned broth (chicken, beef, and vegetable)
- Salad oil
- Olive oil
- Vinegar (distilled white, cider, red wine, balsamic, rice, and/or sherry)
- Rice (long-grain white; arborio or other short-grain white)
- Lentils
- Couscous
- Pasta (small shapes such as orzo; bite-size such as fusilli or penne; long such as spaghetti or capellini)
- All-purpose flour
- Sugar (granulated, brown, powdered)
- Salt
- Baking powder
- Baking soda
- Cream of tartar
- Vanilla and almond extracts
- Cornstarch
- Yellow cornmeal
- Rolled oats
- Raisins
- Semisweet chocolate chips
- Unsweetened cocoa
- Evaporated skim milk
- Coconut milk

IN THE LIQUOR CABINET

- Dry red and white wine
- Dry vermouth

Port
Brandy
Tequila

IN THE PRODUCE BIN
These don't need refrigeration, but they should be kept in a cool, dark, dry place.
Garlic
Onions (yellow and red)
Shallots
Russet potatoes

IN THE REFRIGERATOR
Milk
Sour cream
Plain yogurt
Butter or margarine
Cheese (Parmesan, jack, blue-veined, Swiss or Gruyère)
Eggs
Mayonnaise
Catsup
Mustard (Dijon, coarse-grained)
Salsa
Capers
Prepared horseradish
Lemons
Oranges
Salad greens
Carrots
Celery
Green onions
Parsley
Thin-skinned potatoes
Ginger root
Nuts (pine nuts, sliced almonds, pecans, walnuts)

IN THE FREEZER
Keep out-of-season fruits and vegetables in the freezer, so you'll have them when needed. Breads also keep best when frozen—unless you use them very quickly.
Ice cream or frozen yogurt
Raspberries
Blueberries
Cranberries
Orange juice concentrate
Tiny peas
Breads (firm-textured white, whole wheat, English muffins, bagels, pita)
Bread crumbs (fine dry, plain and seasoned)
Puff pastry
Frozen bread dough
Tortillas (flour, corn)

ON THE SPICE AND HERB SHELVES
Basil (dried)
Bay leaves
Celery seeds
Cinnamon (ground and sticks)
Cloves (ground and whole)
Coriander (ground)
Crushed red pepper flakes
Cumin (ground and seeds)
Curry powder
Fennel seeds
Herbes de Provence
Marjoram
Mustard (dry and seeds)
Nutmeg (ground)
Oregano (dried)
Paprika
Pepper (ground; whole black and green peppercorns)
Rosemary (dried)
Sage (dried)
Tarragon (dried)
Thyme (dried)

By varying the amount and type of curry powder you use, you can give this soup a lightly spicy flavor or a more potent and exciting one. To complete a simple supper, add poached chicken breast halves and toasted split pita breads.

Curried Zucchini & Cilantro Soup

1 medium-size onion
(about 6 oz./170 g)

1 tablespoon (15 ml) olive oil

About 2 pounds (905 g)
zucchini, diced

3 cloves garlic, minced or
pressed

2 teaspoons to 1½ tablespoons
curry powder

1 quart (950 ml) buttermilk

2 cups (470 ml) fat-free
reduced-sodium
chicken broth

¼ cup (10 g) minced cilantro

Plain nonfat yogurt
(optional)

Lime wedges or slices

Cilantro sprigs

Salt

Pepper

Cut onion into quarters; then thinly slice quarters crosswise. Set aside.

Preheat a 4- or 5-quart pan over medium-high heat until rim of pan is hot-to-the-touch. Add oil and wait for about 1 more minute. Add onion, zucchini, and garlic; cook, stirring occasionally, until onion is soft (about 20 minutes).

Stir curry powder into vegetable mixture (the more curry you use, the hotter the soup's flavor will be). Cook, stirring, until curry powder begins to stick to pan bottom (about 5 minutes). Add buttermilk, broth, and minced cilantro; stir to scrape any browned bits free from pan bottom.

Bring soup almost to a boil; remove from heat. Ladle soup into bowls; top with yogurt (if desired), lime, and cilantro sprigs. Season to taste with salt and pepper.

Makes 6 servings

Prep: About 25 minutes
Cook: About 30 minutes

Per serving: 128 calories, 4 g total fat, 1 g saturated fat, 7 mg cholesterol, 365 mg sodium, 16 g carbohydrates, 2 g fiber, 9 g protein, 227 mg calcium, 1 mg iron

Cooking tips: A 4- or 5-quart pan is a good all-purpose size. For a family of four, it's large enough to handle soups and stews, pasta, rice, and boiled artichokes or potatoes.

Accompany this Mexican variation on French onion soup with a platter of boiled or grilled shrimp and a salad of chopped peppers and corn in a cumin-spiked vinaigrette. To conclude a perfect warm-weather meal, offer scoops of chocolate ice cream dusted with cinnamon.

Mexican Onion Soup

6 *large onions (about 3½ lbs./1.6 kg total), thinly sliced*

7½ *cups (1.7 liters) fat-free reduced-sodium chicken broth*

1 *teaspoon ground cumin*

½ *teaspoon ground coriander*

½ *teaspoon dried oregano*

⅓ *cup (40 g) all-purpose flour*

2 *tablespoons chili powder or ground dried New Mexico or California chiles*

6 *corn tortillas (each about 6 inches in diameter)*
   Salad oil

1¼ *cups (about 5 oz./140 g) shredded jalapeño jack cheese*

⅓ *cup (13 g) chopped cilantro*
   Salt

In a 5- or 6-quart pan, combine onions, 1 cup (240 ml) of the broth, cumin, coriander, and oregano. Cook over high heat, stirring occasionally, until almost all liquid has evaporated (about 15 minutes). Then continue to cook, stirring often and scraping browned bits free from pan bottom, until onions are a rich caramel color (about 15 more minutes; watch closely to prevent scorching).

Meanwhile, smoothly mix remaining 6½ cups (1.5 liters) broth with flour. Stir chili powder into onion mixture and cook, stirring, for about 1 minute. Pour broth mixture into pan. Bring to a boil over high heat, stirring. Then reduce heat so soup simmers gently; simmer, uncovered, for 15 minutes to blend flavors, stirring often. Cover and keep warm while making tortilla strips.

To make tortilla strips, stack tortillas and cut into strips about ¼ inch (6 mm) wide. Pour oil into a 3- or 5-quart sauté pan to a depth of about ¼ inch (6 mm). Place over medium heat. When oil registers 350°F (175°C) on a deep-frying thermometer, drop about a fourth of the tortilla strips into oil. Stir until strips are golden and crisp (about 1 minute). Remove from oil with a slotted spoon and drain on paper towels. Repeat to cook remaining tortilla strips.

Ladle soup into bowls and sprinkle with cheese, tortilla strips, and cilantro. Season to taste with salt.

Makes 6 servings

Prep: *About 15 minutes*
Cook: *About 1 hour*

Per serving: *339 calories, 14 g total fat, 5 g saturated fat, 25 mg cholesterol, 910 mg sodium, 42 g carbohydrates, 6 g fiber, 15 g protein, 273 mg calcium, 2 mg iron*

Cooking tips: *To speed preparation, you can substitute purchased tortilla chips for homemade tortilla strips.*

As the main course of a light dinner, this substantial vegetable soup needs only a fresh baguette alongside. For a heartier meal, add a wedge of cheese and a green salad; or let a chicken roast while you prepare the soup.

Cream of Potato & Leek Soup with Bacon

3 medium-size leeks (about
   1⅓ lbs./605 g total)

4 ounces (115 g) sliced bacon,
   chopped

1½ pounds medium-size
   thin-skinned or russet
   potatoes, scrubbed

1½ quarts (1.4 liters)
   fat-free reduced-sodium
   chicken broth

2 cups (470 ml) low-fat
   (2%) milk

1 cup (145 g) diced carrots

8 ounces (230 g) green beans
   (ends trimmed), cut into
   1- to 3-inch (2.5- to 8-cm)
   lengths
   Salt

Trim and discard all but 1½ inches (3.5 cm) of green tops from leeks; split leeks lengthwise and rinse well. Cut leeks into 2-inch (5-cm) matchstick pieces. Set aside.

Preheat a 4- or 5-quart pan over medium-high heat until rim of pan is hot-to-the-touch. Add bacon and cook, stirring occasionally, until crisp (3 to 5 minutes). With a slotted spoon, remove bacon from pan and set aside. Discard drippings from pan. Add two-thirds of the leeks to pan; cook, stirring often, until soft (about 5 minutes).

Meanwhile, peel and dice potatoes; as you dice potatoes, drop them in a bowl of cold water to keep them from turning brown. When all potatoes have been cut, remove two-thirds of them from water; drain, then add to leeks. Stir in broth and milk. Increase heat to high and bring liquid to a boil; then reduce heat, cover, and simmer until potatoes mash easily (about 10 minutes).

With a slotted spoon, remove vegetables from broth and transfer to a food processor or blender (if using a blender, add some of the broth). Process just until coarsely puréed; whisk back into broth. Return to a boil; then reduce heat so soup simmers.

Drain remaining potatoes and add them to soup along with carrots. Return to a simmer; cover and cook for 4 minutes. Add beans, cover, and cook for 4 minutes. Reserve a few leek slivers for garnish; add remaining leeks and bacon to pan. Continue to cook until potatoes and carrots are soft and beans are tender-crisp to bite but still bright green (2 to 3 more minutes). Ladle soup into bowls; garnish with leek slivers. Season to taste with salt.

Makes 8 servings

Prep: *About 25 minutes*
Cook: *About 30 minutes*

Per serving: *167 calories, 3 g total fat, 1 g saturated fat, 8 mg cholesterol, 534 mg sodium, 26 g carbohydrates, 3 g fiber, 8 g protein, 108 mg calcium, 2 mg iron*

Served with crusty French bread and a fresh fruit plate, a bowl of this soup makes a satisfying lunch. For the fruit, choose cubed mangoes and small bunches of green grapes; or offer juicy pineapple rings sprinkled with cilantro leaves. At dinner time, you might add sliced ham to the menu.

Black Bean Soup

1   *tablespoon (15 ml) olive oil*

2   *medium-size onions (about 12 oz./340 g total), chopped*

6   *cloves garlic, minced or pressed*

1/2   *teaspoon ground cumin*

3   *cans (about 15 oz./425 g each) black beans, drained and rinsed*

1   *can (about 14 1/2 oz./415 g) stewed pear-shaped tomatoes with onion, celery, and green bell pepper*

1   *tablespoon minced cilantro*

1/2   *teaspoon dried oregano*

3   *cups (710 ml) fat-free reduced-sodium chicken broth*

   Reduced-fat sour cream

   Lemon slices

   Cilantro sprigs

   Salt

   Pepper

Preheat an 8-quart pan over medium-high heat until rim of pan is hot-to-the-touch. Add oil and wait for about 1 more minute. Then add onions and garlic; cook, stirring occasionally, for 5 minutes. Add cumin and continue to cook, stirring occasionally, until onions are pale golden (about 5 more minutes). Stir in beans, tomatoes (break up with a spoon), minced cilantro, and oregano; remove from heat.

Spoon bean mixture into a food processor or blender, a portion at a time, and process until very coarsely puréed (you should still have some whole beans). Return purée to cooking pan. Stir in broth and bring to a boil over medium-high heat.

Ladle soup into bowls; top with sour cream, lemon, and cilantro sprigs. Season to taste with salt and pepper.

Makes 6 to 8 servings

Prep: *10 to 15 minutes*
Cook: *About 15 minutes*

Per serving: *161 calories, 3 g total fat, .35 g saturated fat, 0 mg cholesterol, 794 mg sodium, 26 g carbohydrates, 7 g fiber, 9 g protein, 63 mg calcium, 2 mg iron*

Cooking tips: *To cut a mango, hold the fruit in one hand with its narrower edge facing you. Slowly cut mango lengthwise down one side of pit until fleshy cheek is completely cut off. Repeat on other side. Score flesh of both cheeks almost to peel in a diamond pattern. Then hold each scored cheek, flesh side up, in your hands; gently push up from below center of mango with your fingertips while the heels of your hands push the edges down and out.*

This red-and-yellow tomato salad is a great partner for Sautéed Steak with Mushrooms (page 44) and baked potatoes. Drink steam beer or iced raspberry tea with your meal; try Apple-Blueberry Crisp (page 88) for dessert.

Mixed Tomato Salad with Arugula & Sage

3 to 3½ pounds (1.3 to 1.6 kg) firm-ripe tomatoes (use half each red and yellow tomatoes, or all red tomatoes)

8 ounces (230 g) red cherry tomatoes

8 ounces (230 g) yellow cherry tomatoes

4 ounces (115 g) arugula or watercress, rinsed and crisped

2 tablespoons minced fresh sage or 2 teaspoons dried rubbed sage

⅓ cup (80 ml) balsamic or sherry vinegar

2 tablespoons (30 ml) extra-virgin olive oil or salad oil

Sage sprigs

Salt

Slice large tomatoes crosswise and arrange on a large rimmed platter. Arrange whole red and yellow cherry tomatoes and arugula over sliced tomatoes; sprinkle with minced sage. In a small bowl, mix vinegar and oil; pour over salad. Garnish with sage sprigs. Season to taste with salt.

Makes 6 to 8 servings

Prep: *About 10 minutes*

Per serving: *96 calories, 5 g total fat, .7 g saturated fat, 0 mg cholesterol, 32 mg sodium, 13 g carbohydrates, 4 g fiber, 3 g protein, 36 mg calcium, 1 mg iron*

Cooking tips: *Extra-virgin olive oil is the free-flowing oil that comes from the first cold pressing of the ripe olives and has an acidity rating of less than 1 percent. It's a higher-quality oil than that derived from later pressings.*

This sophisticated take on old-fashioned wilted lettuce combines three kinds of greens with sweet sliced pears and a hot herbed bacon dressing. Top with toasted pecan halves, if you like, and serve with a wedge of fontina cheese.

Winter Greens with Pears & Warm Bacon Dressing

1 small head romaine lettuce (about 8 oz./230 g), rinsed, crisped, and torn into pieces

1 large head Belgian endive (about 4 oz./115 g), separated into spears, rinsed, and crisped

1 small head radicchio (about 5 oz./140 g), rinsed, crisped, and thinly sliced

4 ounces (115 g) sliced bacon, diced

1 small red onion (about 6 oz./170 g), diced

¼ teaspoon pepper

¼ teaspoon celery seeds

⅛ teaspoon dried rosemary

⅛ teaspoon dried thyme

⅛ teaspoon dry mustard

½ cup (120 ml) cider vinegar

¼ cup (60 ml) balsamic vinegar

¼ cup (55 g) firmly packed brown sugar

¼ cup (60 ml) salad oil

Salt

2 medium-size ripe pears such as Bartlett, Comice, or Anjou (about 1 lb./455 g total)

Toasted pecan halves (optional)

In a large bowl, mix romaine lettuce, endive, and radicchio. Set aside.

To make dressing, preheat a 2-quart sauté pan or 10-inch omelette pan over medium-high heat until rim of pan is hot-to-the-touch. Add bacon and cook, stirring often, until crisp (3 to 5 minutes). Stir in onion, pepper, celery seeds, rosemary, thyme, and mustard. Cook, stirring often, until onion is gold around edges (2 to 3 minutes). Add cider vinegar, balsamic vinegar, and sugar. Bring to a boil; then remove from heat and stir in oil. Season to taste with salt.

Peel and core pears; cut into thin wedges. Mix pears into greens; then transfer salad to a rimmed platter or large salad bowl. Pour warm dressing over salad and mix. Garnish with pecan halves, if desired. Serve at once.

Makes 6 servings

Prep: *About 15 minutes*
Cook: *About 10 minutes*

Per serving: *278 calories, 20 g total fat, 5 g saturated fat, 13 mg cholesterol, 142 mg sodium, 23 g carbohydrates, 3 g fiber, 3 g protein, 54 mg calcium, 2 mg iron*

Cooking tips: *To toast pecan halves, spread them in a cake pan or other shallow baking pan and bake in a 350°F (175°C) oven until nuts just begin to turn darker in color (8 to 10 minutes).*

This chunky red potato salad lends itself perfectly to homey cold-weather menus. Serve it with sautéed sausages and bell peppers and a loaf of pumpernickel or crusty French bread. Beer or sparkling cider is great alongside. For dessert, offer ripe pears and squares of chocolate.

Honey Mustard Potato Salad with Cumin

2½ pounds (1.15 kg) medium-size red thin-skinned potatoes, scrubbed

½ cup (85 g) chopped red onion

1½ cups (180 g) thinly sliced celery

½ cup (120 ml) cider vinegar

3 tablespoons (45 ml) honey

2 tablespoons (30 ml) Dijon mustard

2 teaspoons cumin seeds

Salt

Pepper

In a 4- or 5-quart pan, bring about 2 quarts (1.9 liters) water to a boil over high heat. Add unpeeled potatoes; reduce heat, cover, and simmer until potatoes are tender throughout when pierced (20 to 30 minutes). Drain and immerse in cold water until cool enough to touch; then drain again and cut into about ¾-inch (2-cm) chunks.

Rinse onion with cool running water; drain well. In a large bowl, combine potatoes, onion, and celery. In a small bowl, mix vinegar, honey, mustard, and cumin seeds; pour over salad. Mix well; season to taste with salt and pepper.

Makes 6 servings

Prep: *About 20 minutes*
Cook: *25 to 35 minutes*

Per serving: 206 calories, 1 g total fat, .01 g saturated fat, 0 mg cholesterol, 164 mg sodium, 46 g carbohydrates, 4 g fiber, 4 g protein, 24 mg calcium, 2 mg iron

Cooking tips: This salad has a tangy-sweet flavor similar to that of a hot German potato salad. Reduce the quantity of honey if you prefer a more traditional, less sweet flavor. Use thin-skinned potatoes in salads; they have a waxy texture and keep their shape when diced and mixed with other ingredients. Russets, on the other hand, have a mealy consistency that makes them perfect for mashed potatoes and soups.

Accompany this full-meal salad with a simple combination of oranges and sliced jicama; or try ripe mango, scored and sprinkled with lime juice and salt. Sauvignon blanc or limeade suits the menu nicely. A good choice for dessert is Quick Chocolate Cake (page 95).

Pan-grilled Chicken Salad with Tortilla Chips

1½   cups (360 ml) orange juice

1¼   cups (300 ml) lime juice

⅓   cup (60 g) minced shallots

1¾   teaspoons sugar

½   cup (20 g) chopped cilantro

1½   teaspoons crushed red pepper flakes

1½   teaspoons cumin seeds

2   cloves garlic, minced

6   boneless, skinless chicken breast halves (5 oz./140 g each)

1   medium-size red onion (about 8 oz./230 g), thickly sliced

2   cans (about 15 oz./425 g each) black beans, drained and rinsed

1   large red bell pepper (8 oz./ 230 g), seeded and chopped

4   teaspoons (20 ml) salad oil

3   quarts (660 g) finely shredded romaine lettuce

6   to 8 cups purchased baked tortilla chips
    Reduced-fat sour cream

1   medium-size firm-ripe avocado (about 10 oz./285 g), pitted, peeled, and thinly sliced
    Cilantro sprigs
    Salt

In a bowl, mix orange juice, lime juice, shallots, sugar, chopped cilantro, red pepper flakes, cumin seeds, and garlic.

Rinse chicken, pat dry, and place in a large plastic food bag; add ⅓ cup (80 ml) of the dressing. Seal bag and rotate to coat chicken with dressing; set bag in a bowl. Place onion in another plastic food bag with another ⅓ cup (80 ml) of the dressing. Seal bag and rotate to mix; set in bowl with chicken. Let chicken and onion stand for 10 to 15 minutes, turning bags over occasionally.

Drain dressing from onion into a measuring cup and add enough of the remaining dressing to make ½ cup (120 ml). Pour this dressing into a large bowl; mix in beans and bell pepper. Set bean salad aside.

Drain and discard dressing from chicken. Preheat a grill pan over medium-high heat until rim of pan is hot-to-the-touch. Add 2 teaspoons of the oil and wait for about 1 more minute. Then add chicken and cook, turning as needed, until chicken is browned on both sides and no longer pink in thickest part; cut to test (8 to 10 minutes). Remove to a platter and keep warm. Heat remaining 2 teaspoons oil in pan; add onion slices and cook, turning as needed, until flecked with brown on both sides (about 3 minutes). Transfer onion to platter.

To serve, slice chicken and separate onion slices into rings. Mound lettuce on 6 individual plates; top with bean salad. Then top each serving with one sliced chicken breast and one-sixth of the onion rings. Tuck tortilla chips around salads; garnish with sour cream, avocado, and cilantro sprigs. Season to taste with remaining dressing and salt.

Makes 6 servings

Prep: *About 15 minutes, plus 10 to 15 minutes to marinate*
Cook: *About 15 minutes*

Per serving: *624 calories, 14 g total fat, 2 g saturated fat, 82 mg cholesterol, 351 mg sodium, 79 g carbohydrates, 10 g fiber, 48 g protein, 312 mg calcium, 5 mg iron*

This summery dish is ideal for a patio picnic. Try it with grilled lamb chops or barbecued steak, corn on the cob, and a pitcher of iced black or herbal tea. For dessert, serve scoops of vanilla or peach ice cream topped with honey and pistachios.

Orzo with Mint & Tomato

1   tablespoon (15 ml) olive oil

1   large onion (about
    8 oz./230 g), chopped

1½ cups (300 g) dried orzo

¼   cup (60 ml) fat-free
    reduced-sodium chicken
    broth

3   tablespoons (45 ml) lemon
    juice

2   to 4 tablespoons minced
    parsley

1   large tomato (about
    8 oz./230 g), chopped

¼   to ½ cup (10 to 20 g)
    minced fresh mint

2   tablespoons drained capers
    (optional)

    Mint sprigs

    Lemon wedges

    Salt

    Pepper

Preheat a 10- or 12-inch omelette pan over medium-high heat until rim of pan is hot-to-the-touch. Add oil and wait for about 1 more minute. Add onion and cook, stirring often, until onion is browned and tastes sweet (about 10 minutes).

Meanwhile, in a 4- or 5-quart pan, bring about 1½ quarts (1.4 liters) water to a boil over high heat. Add pasta and cook, uncovered, until al dente (6 to 8 minutes). Drain, rinse with cold water until cool, and drain again.

In a medium-size bowl, combine pasta, onion, broth, lemon juice, and parsley. Add tomato, minced mint, and capers (if desired); stir gently to mix. Garnish with mint sprigs. Season to taste with lemon, salt, and pepper.

Makes 4 to 6 servings

Prep: *About 20 minutes*
Cook: *About 15 minutes*

Per serving: *276 calories, 4 g total fat, 1 g saturated fat, 0 mg cholesterol, 40 mg sodium, 51 g carbohydrates, 3 g fiber, 9 g protein, 30 mg calcium, 3 mg iron*

Cooking tips: *Equally flavorful substitutions for pungent mint include fresh cilantro and basil. Or use a smaller quantity of fresh dill.*

To cook pasta properly, bring a large, covered pot of water to a rapid boil. Then add the pasta and cook, uncovered, until al dente ("to the tooth")—cooked through but still slightly chewy. To drain, lift out the pasta insert, if you used one; or pour the pasta into a colander. Leave a few tablespoons of cooking water in the pasta to keep the strands or pieces from sticking together.

If you like, surround this hearty, sausage-sauced pasta with small spinach leaves dressed in a simple blend of olive oil, lemon juice, salt, and pepper. Enjoy a glass of red wine alongside; or end the meal with Italian mint or lemon syrup splashed into sparkling water and ice.

Italian Fusilli

12 ounces (340 g) dried fusilli

8 ounces (230 g) mild or hot turkey Italian sausage

2 cans (about 14½ oz./425 g each) sliced stewed Italian-style tomatoes

2 teaspoons fennel seeds

1 cup (40 g) chopped fresh basil

Basil sprigs

Grated Asiago or Parmesan cheese

Salt

Pepper

Fill an 8-quart stock pot three-fourths full of water; cover and bring to a boil over high heat. Then add pasta and cook, uncovered, until al dente (about 10 minutes).

Meanwhile, preheat a 10- or 12-inch omelette pan over medium-high heat until rim of pan is hot-to-the-touch. Squeeze sausage from casings into pan; cook, stirring to break meat into chunks, until meat is browned (about 6 minutes). Stir in tomatoes (break up any large slices with a spoon) and fennel seeds. Reduce heat and simmer, uncovered, for 5 minutes. Stir in chopped basil.

Drain pasta and return to pan. Add tomato-sausage sauce and toss to mix with pasta. Spoon onto a platter or plates; garnish with basil sprigs and sprinkle with cheese. Season to taste with salt and pepper.

Makes 4 servings

Prep: *Concurrent with cooking*
Cook: *About 20 minutes*

Per serving: *495 calories, 8 g total fat, 2 g saturated fat, 30 mg cholesterol, 1,100 mg sodium, 84 g carbohydrates, 7 g fiber, 23 g protein, 135 mg calcium, 7 mg iron*

Cooking tips: *When you use a nonstick pan, you can often completely eliminate the fat in a recipe. This simple sausage sauce for pasta is a good example: the meat browns nicely from the dry heat, and the small amount of fat it contains adds a little succulence.*

Finish off this simple meal with a luscious dessert. Make Almond Cake with Stewed Fruit (page 91); or spoon fresh blueberries and raspberries over cubed angel food cake, drench with marsala wine, and top with softly whipped cream and a dusting of cocoa.

Lemon-Garlic-Pepper Shrimp with Angel Hair Pasta

2 *tablespoons (30 ml) olive oil*

4 *cloves garlic, minced or pressed*

1 *large yellow bell pepper (about 8 oz./230 g), seeded and diced*

1 *large red bell pepper (about 8 oz./230 g), seeded and diced*

2 *medium-size ripe tomatoes (about ⅔ lb./285 g total), chopped*

8 *ounces (230 g) dried angel hair pasta (capellini)*

1 *pound (455 g) tiny cooked shrimp*

1 *teaspoon grated lemon zest*

Salt

Pepper

Italian parsley sprigs

Grated Parmesan cheese

Preheat a 3- or 5-quart sauté pan over medium-high heat until rim of pan is hot-to-the-touch. Add oil and wait for about 1 more minute. Add garlic and stir until it begins to color (about 30 seconds). Add yellow and red bell peppers and cook, stirring occasionally, until some of the edges begin to brown slightly (about 8 minutes). Stir in tomatoes. When liquid begins to boil, reduce heat and simmer until tomatoes fall apart and form a sauce (about 5 minutes).

Meanwhile, fill a 3- or 4-quart pan three-fourths full of water; cover and bring to a boil over high heat. Add pasta and cook, uncovered, until al dente (about 3 minutes). Drain, pour onto a platter, and keep hot.

Stir shrimp and lemon zest into sauce; simmer just until shrimp are heated through (about 5 minutes). Season to taste with salt and pepper. Pour sauce over pasta. Garnish with parsley sprigs and sprinkle with cheese.

Makes 4 servings

Prep: *About 20 minutes*
Cook: *About 20 minutes*

Per serving: *428 calories, 9 g total fat, 1 g saturated fat, 221 mg cholesterol, 267 mg sodium, 53 g carbohydrates, 4 g fiber, 33 g protein, 73 mg calcium, 7 mg iron*

Cooking tips: *Citrus zest, valued for its fresh fragrance and intense flavor, is the colored part of the fruit's peel. The white membrane beneath the zest is bitter tasting, so it's best not to use it in cooking. To remove the zest, use a citrus zester to shave off thin strips; or, for grated zest, carefully rub the whole fruit over a grater.*

Using a pasta insert lets you drain pasta more safely and efficiently. The insert can also be used for making stocks and broths and for cooking seafood or corn on the cob. It comes in handy for canning, too, making it easy to lift jars from a boiling water bath.

To round out the meal, add a leafy mixed salad, crusty Italian bread to spread with pesto, and a good red wine. For dessert, mix soft vanilla ice cream with candied orange peel, almonds, coconut, and chopped chocolate; spoon into bowls and drizzle with rum.

Penne with Sun-dried Tomatoes, Asparagus & Pine Nuts

3   ounces (85 g) sun-dried
    tomatoes

2   cups (470 ml) water

1   pound (455 g) dried
    tube-shaped pasta such as
    penne, mostaccioli, or ziti

12 ounces (340 g) asparagus,
    tough ends snapped off, spears
    cut diagonally into 2- to
    3-inch (5- to 8-cm) lengths

2   tablespoons (30 ml) olive oil

⅔   cup (85 g) pine nuts

2   shallots, minced

4   cloves garlic, minced or
    pressed

¼   cup (10 g) slivered or
    chopped fresh basil

1   cup (about 3 oz./85 g) grated
    Parmesan cheese

    Basil sprigs

    Curls of Parmesan cheese

    Pepper

In a 2- or 3-quart pan, combine sun-dried tomatoes and the 2 cups (470 ml) water. Bring to a boil over high heat; then reduce heat and simmer, uncovered, until liquid is reduced to ¾ to 1 cup (180 to 240 ml) and tomatoes are soft (about 10 minutes). With a slotted spoon, remove tomatoes from pan. Chop tomatoes and return them to cooking liquid; set aside.

While tomatoes are cooking, fill a 6- or 8-quart pan three-fourths full of water; cover and bring to a boil over high heat. Add pasta and cook, uncovered, for 5 minutes. Add asparagus to boiling water with pasta; continue to cook, uncovered, until asparagus is barely tender when pierced and pasta is al dente (5 to 7 more minutes). Drain well and keep hot.

Preheat a 13-inch paella pan or 3- or 5-quart sauté pan over medium heat until rim of pan is hot-to-the-touch. Add oil and wait for about 1 more minute. Add pine nuts, shallots, and garlic; cook, stirring, until shallots are translucent (about 4 minutes). Add pasta, asparagus, sun-dried tomatoes and their liquid, and slivered basil. Stir pasta mixture just until hot. Mix in grated cheese.

Serve pasta from pan or pour onto a platter. Garnish with basil sprigs and curls of cheese; season to taste with pepper.

Makes 6 servings

Prep: *About 15 minutes*
Cook: *About 25 minutes*

Per serving: *518 calories, 18 g total fat, 4 g saturated fat, 10 mg cholesterol, 249 mg sodium, 71 g carbohydrates, 7 g fiber, 23 g protein, 216 mg calcium, 5 mg iron*

Cooking tips: *To make thin shavings of Parmesan cheese that curl slightly, bring a chunk of cheese to room temperature; then slowly pull a vegetable peeler across it.*

Here's a good choice for a meatless meal. Serve the risotto with lemon wedges and a bowl of freshly grated Parmesan cheese; add a crisp salad alongside. Choose a light dessert, perhaps green grapes with almond macaroons and coffee or milk.

Risotto with Mushrooms & Asparagus

1 tablespoon (15 ml) olive oil

4 ounces (115 g) sliced mushrooms

1 cup (170 g) diced onion

1 cup (185 g) arborio or long-grain white rice

3½ to 4 cups (830 to 950 ml) fat-free reduced-sodium chicken broth

1 teaspoon dried thyme

8 spears asparagus, tough ends snapped off, spears cut into 1-inch (2.5-cm) lengths

Salt

Pepper

Preheat a 4- or 5-quart pan over medium heat until rim of pan is hot-to-the-touch. Add oil and wait for about 1 more minute. Add mushrooms and onion. Cook, stirring often, until vegetables soften and begin to stick to pan bottom (about 15 minutes). Add water, 1 tablespoon (15 ml) at a time, if pan drippings begin to scorch.

Add rice and stir until opaque (3 to 4 minutes). Stir in broth and thyme; bring to a boil, stirring often. Then reduce heat and simmer, uncovered, until rice is tender to bite and almost all liquid has been absorbed (about 25 minutes); stir occasionally at first, more often as mixture thickens. About 5 minutes before rice is done, stir in asparagus.

Season risotto to taste with salt and pepper.

Makes 6 servings

Prep: *About 5 minutes*
Cook: *About 45 minutes*

Per serving: *162 calories, 3 g total fat, .36 g saturated fat, 0 mg cholesterol, 354 mg sodium, 29 g carbohydrates, 1 g fiber, 5 g protein, 24 mg calcium, 2 mg iron*

Cooking tips: *Arborio rice is a medium-grain rice. As it cooks, it releases more starch than does long-grain white rice, giving the dishes in which it is used a creamier texture. Heavy-gauge aluminum conducts heat so evenly that risotto made in Calphalon pans cook beautifully, with very little chance of scorching.*

Let this fragrant Thai-style rice be the centerpiece of a colorful buffet meal. Mound the rice on a platter; then surround it with side dishes such as skewered grilled chicken, tiny shrimp, baby corn, sliced bell peppers and cucumbers, and perhaps pineapple and banana slices with cilantro.

Coconut Rice

2 tablespoons (30 ml) salad oil

3 cloves garlic, minced or pressed

1 tablespoon minced fresh ginger

3 cups (555 g) long-grain white rice

2 cups (470 ml) canned low-fat coconut milk

3 cups (710 ml) fat-free reduced-sodium chicken broth

3 green onions, sliced diagonally

  Lime wedges

Preheat a 13-inch paella pan or 3- or 5-quart sauté pan over medium-high heat until rim of pan is hot-to-the-touch. Add oil and wait for about 1 more minute. Add garlic and ginger; cook, stirring, until garlic starts to color (1 to 2 minutes).

Add rice and stir until opaque (2 to 3 minutes). Add coconut milk and broth, stirring to scrape browned bits free from pan bottom. Bring to a boil; then reduce heat, cover, and simmer until liquid has been absorbed and rice is tender to bite (about 20 minutes). Fluff rice with a fork and sprinkle with onions. Garnish with lime.

Makes 8 servings

Prep: *About 10 minutes*
Cook: *About 25 minutes*

Per serving: *353 calories, 6 g total fat, 3 g saturated fat, 0 mg cholesterol, 235 mg sodium, 60 g carbohydrates, 1 g fiber, 6 g protein, 26 mg calcium, 3 mg iron*

Cooking tips: *Preheating your pan until the rim is hot-to-the-touch lets you know that the pan bottom has reached the proper cooking temperature. When food is added, it will sear, sealing in juices, and will brown and crisp more evenly, with less chance of sticking.*

Canned low-fat coconut milk is a good alternative to the regular (full-fat) variety. For an even lower-fat substitute, add ½ to 1 teaspoon coconut extract to every 2 cups (470 ml) whole milk.

Serve these special-occasion steaks with warm, crisp-crusted Italian bread and a tossed salad or Mixed Tomato Salad with Arugula & Sage (page 23). Thin slices of pound cake topped with berries in orange liqueur complete a luxurious meal.

Steak with Peppercorns

2 tablespoons whole black peppercorns (or use 2 teaspoons each black peppercorns, dried green peppercorns, and pink peppercorns)

4 beef tenderloin (fillet) steaks, each about 1 inch (2.5 cm) thick (about 7 oz./200 g each)

1 tablespoon (15 ml) olive oil

1 cup (240 ml) cognac or other brandy

1 cup (240 ml) fat-free reduced-sodium beef broth

2 tablespoons (30 ml) Dijon mustard

½ cup (120 ml) evaporated skim milk or whipping cream
Salt

In a clean coffee grinder, coarsely grind peppercorns. Or coarsely crush peppercorns, using a mortar and pestle; or crush on a cutting board using the bottom of a heavy sauce pan.

Coat both sides of each steak evenly with ground peppercorns, using your hand to press peppercorns firmly into meat.

Preheat a 2- or 3-quart sauté pan over medium-high heat until rim of pan is hot-to-the-touch. Add oil and wait for about 1 more minute. Then add steaks and cook, turning once, until meat is done rare; cut to test (10 to 12 minutes). Remove steaks to a plate and keep warm while you make sauce.

To make sauce, pour cognac and broth into sauté pan, stirring to scrape browned bits free from pan bottom. Whisk in mustard and milk. Bring to a boil over high heat; then boil, uncovered, until reduced to 1¼ cups/300 ml (10 to 15 minutes). Pour sauce over steaks. Season to taste with salt.

Makes 4 servings

Prep: *About 10 minutes*
Cook: *25 to 30 minutes*

Per serving: *629 calories, 43 g total fat, 16 g saturated fat, 122 mg cholesterol, 457 mg sodium, 6 g carbohydrates, 1 g fiber, 34 g protein, 118 mg calcium, 5 mg iron*

Cooking tips: *Evaporated skim milk is a low-fat alternative to whipping cream. Sauces made with it will be slightly thinner and less shiny than those made with cream.*

Big, juicy steaks crowned with garlicky sautéed mushrooms are so satisfying that you can keep the rest of the meal very simple: crusty French rolls, crumb-topped broiled tomato halves, and a robust red wine.

Sautéed Steak with Mushrooms

4 New York strip steaks, each
  about 1 inch (2.5 cm) thick
  (about 8 oz./230 g each)

1½ tablespoons (23 ml) olive oil

8 large cloves garlic, minced
  or pressed

1 pound (455 g) mushrooms,
  sliced

½ cup (120 ml) dry red wine,
  such as cabernet sauvignon
  or merlot

½ cup (120 ml) fat-free
  reduced-sodium beef broth

1½ teaspoons dried rosemary

  Rosemary sprigs

  Salt

  Pepper

If serving 8 people, cut each steak in half.

Preheat a 3- or 5-quart sauté pan or 10- or 12-inch omelette pan over medium-high heat until rim of pan is hot-to-the-touch. Add oil and wait for about 1 more minute. Place steaks in pan and cook, turning once, until meat is done rare; cut to test (10 to 12 minutes). Transfer to a plate and keep warm.

Add garlic to pan. Reduce heat to medium and stir garlic for 30 seconds. Then add mushrooms, increase heat to medium-high, and cook, stirring occasionally, until liquid has evaporated and mushrooms are well browned (12 to 15 minutes).

Pour wine and broth over mushrooms; sprinkle with dried rosemary. Stir to scrape browned bits free from pan bottom. Bring to a boil over high heat; then boil, uncovered, until liquid is reduced by half (about 5 minutes). Pour mushroom mixture over steaks, garnish with rosemary sprigs, and serve at once. Season to taste with salt and pepper.

Makes 4 large or 8 small servings

Prep: *About 5 minutes*
Cook: *About 35 minutes*

Per large serving: *661 calories, 46 g total fat, 17 g saturated fat, 152 mg cholesterol, 206 mg sodium, 9 g carbohydrates, 2 g fiber, 46 g protein, 41 mg calcium, 5 mg iron*

Cooking tips: *Sauté pans are a great choice for sautéing, braising, and frying; they make deglazing easy, too. They have a wide, flat bottom to provide the greatest possible cooking surface; their sides are high and straight, to hold in liquid easily and keep oil from spattering. And because they come with lids, they're ideal for covered simmering.*

3

...anks ...ssed.
"..."
... kn.w. Why
...add, standing

... water, neat as
...m of something
... or striped. Tiger,
...ian. There he was,
...Maries de la Mer. He
...She bobbed up at his

...t Provence itself exactly.
...elf."

...e boat. They did not play
...me close on a corner as he
...rope, and under the colorless
...brushed weightlessly. It was
...n thought, she with greed and
...nse of injury, and an animal
...ething he couldn't catch.

...us hootings and echoings. I heard

This simplified version of the famous Belgian carbonnade simmers to tenderness on top of the stove. Serve with dark rye bread and buttered egg noodles or mashed potatoes; offer juicy ripe pears and Gruyère cheese for dessert.

Belgian Beer Stew

4   ounces (115 g) sliced bacon, diced

1   pound (455 g) onions, thinly sliced

1½ pounds (680 g) boneless beef chuck, trimmed of fat and cut into 1- by 2-inch chunks

    About ¼ cup (30 g) all-purpose flour

1½ teaspoons butter or margarine

1½ teaspoons salad oil

1   teaspoon sugar

1   teaspoon red or white wine vinegar

1   thick slice rye bread

1   tablespoon (15 ml) Dijon mustard

1   bottle (about 12 oz./340 g) dark beer

    Chopped Italian parsley and Italian parsley sprigs

    Salt

Preheat a 10- or 12-inch omelette pan or 3- or 5-quart sauté pan over medium heat until rim of pan is hot-to-the-touch. Add bacon and cook, stirring occasionally, until crisp (5 to 6 minutes). With a slotted spoon, remove bacon from pan and set aside. Add onions to drippings in pan. Reduce heat to low and cook, turning onions often with a wide spatula, until onions are soft and pale golden (20 to 30 minutes).

Meanwhile, coat beef with flour and shake off excess. Preheat a 5-quart saucier or 4- or 5-quart pan over medium-high heat until rim of pan is hot-to-the-touch. Add butter and oil and wait for about 1 more minute. Then add meat and cook, turning as needed, until browned on all sides (about 10 minutes).

Add onions, sugar, and vinegar to meat. Spread bread with mustard and place, mustard side up, atop meat mixture. Pour beer over bread and meat. Bring to a boil; then reduce heat, cover, and simmer until meat is tender when pierced (45 minutes to 1 hour). Sprinkle stew with bacon; garnish with parsley. Season to taste with salt.

Makes 4 servings

Prep: *About 10 minutes*
Cook: *1¼ to 1½ hours*

Per serving: *560 calories, 33 g total fat, 12 g saturated fat, 134 mg cholesterol, 508 mg sodium, 25 g carbohydrates, 3 g fiber, 39 g protein, 56 mg calcium, 5 mg iron*

Cooking tips: *This stew's flavor depends on the type of beer you use. Darker varieties give a more intense beer flavor, with an interesting, slightly bitter hint of hops.*

Garnish these lavishly glazed ribs with thin-sliced cucumbers, whole green onions, and a fan of yellow or orange bell pepper strips. Accompany with fluffy white rice. To close the meal, try a bowl of boysenberries and sliced nectarines drenched in a chilled muscat dessert wine.

Shanghai-style Sweet-Sour Ribs

3   pounds (1.35 kg) pork spareribs, cut across the bone into 1½-inch (3.5-cm) lengths

½   cup (100 g) sugar

⅓   cup (80 ml) Chinese black vinegar or balsamic vinegar

1   tablespoon (15 ml) dark soy sauce (or 2½ teaspoons soy sauce plus ½ teaspoon dark molasses)

3   cloves garlic, minced or pressed

    Salt

Cut ribs between bones to separate; then place ribs in an 11- by 14-inch or 13- by 16-inch roasting pan. Bake, uncovered, in a 450°F (230°C) oven, stirring often, until well browned (about 30 minutes). Remove ribs from pan and drain on paper towels; keep warm.

In a wok or 10- or 12-inch omelette pan, mix sugar, vinegar, soy sauce, and garlic. Bring to a boil over high heat. Reduce heat to medium; cook, uncovered, stirring often, until sauce is reduced to about ½ cup/120 ml (8 to 10 minutes). Add ribs to sauce and stir to coat. Pour ribs and sauce onto a platter; serve warm or at room temperature. Season to taste with salt.

Makes 4 servings

Prep: *About 10 minutes*
Cook: *About 40 minutes*

Per serving: *634 calories, 40 g total fat, 15 g saturated fat, 161 mg cholesterol, 255 mg sodium, 27 g carbohydrates, .04 g fiber, 39 g protein, 71 mg calcium, 3 mg iron*

Cooking tips: *Have the ribs for this recipe cut crosswise into pieces for you at the meat market. Garnish the dish as the photo shows; or use cucumbers alone, cut into paper-thin slices and arranged in a thick border all around the ribs.*

Grilled peach halves and a watercress salad with toasted pecans enhance these richly sauced pork tenderloins. For dessert, offer hot espresso and small scoops of hazelnut or toasted almond ice cream sprinkled with finely crushed purchased nut brittle.

Pork Tenderloin with Stilton & Port

1   tablespoon (15 ml) salad oil

2   or 3 pork tenderloins
    (about 1¹/₂ lbs./680 g total),
    trimmed of fat

1   cup (240 ml) port

¹/₂ cup (120 ml) fat-free
    reduced-sodium
    chicken broth

¹/₂ cup (120 ml) evaporated
    skim milk or
    whipping cream

4   ounces (115 g) Stilton
    cheese, crumbled

1   or 2 fresh jalapeño chiles,
    seeded and diced (optional)

Preheat a 3- or 5-quart sauté pan over medium-high heat until rim of pan is hot-to-the-touch. Add oil and wait for about 1 more minute. Add pork and cook, turning as needed, until browned on all sides (about 4 minutes).

Transfer meat to a 9- by 13-inch baking pan and bake in a 400°F (205°C) oven until a meat thermometer inserted in thickest part of tenderloin registers 160°F/71°C (about 15 minutes).

Meanwhile, discard fat from sauté pan and add port and broth. Bring to a boil over high heat; then boil, uncovered, until reduced to about ³/₄ cup/180 ml (about 3 minutes). Stir in milk and continue to boil, stirring, until sauce is covered with large, shiny bubbles (about 5 more minutes). Add cheese and stir until melted; stir in chiles, if desired. Remove from heat.

To serve, thinly slice meat across the grain. Fan out slices on individual plates and spoon sauce over them.

Makes 4 to 6 servings

Prep: *About 10 minutes*
Cook: *About 20 minutes*

Per serving: *362 calories, 14 g total fat, 6 g saturated fat, 107 mg cholesterol, 474 mg sodium, 9 g carbohydrates, 0 g fiber, 36 g protein, 204 mg calcium, 2 mg iron*

Cooking tips: *If you like bold flavors, include the jalapeño chiles in this recipe; if you prefer a milder dish, try garnishing meat and sauce with minced parsley and additional small chunks of Stilton cheese.*

Accompany this hearty oven supper with garlic toast and thickly sliced tomatoes with basil leaves. Crisp apples or ripe pears served with warm roasted almonds or walnuts round out the menu nicely.

Mustard-crusted Lamb Chops with Potatoes

2 tablespoons (30 ml) olive oil

4 large red thin-skinned potatoes (about 2 lbs./ 905 g total), scrubbed and thickly sliced

¼ cup (60 ml) Dijon mustard

2 teaspoons mustard seeds

½ to 1 teaspoon pepper

4 loin lamb chops, each about 2 inches (5 cm) thick (about 1½ lbs./680 g total)

¼ cup (11 g) Italian-seasoned fine dry bread crumbs

Italian parsley sprigs (optional)

Pour oil into an 11- by 14-inch roasting pan. Place pan in a 450°F (230°C) oven and heat for about 30 seconds. Remove pan from oven and add potatoes, turning slices to coat with oil on all sides. Bake until golden and crisp on the outside, soft on the inside (about 45 minutes), turning every 15 minutes.

Meanwhile, in a small bowl, mix mustard, mustard seeds, and pepper; set aside. Trim and discard fat from chops; place chops in another lightly oiled 11- by 14-inch roasting pan.

When potatoes are almost done, move them to lowest oven rack. Reset oven to broil. Broil chops 4 to 6 inches (10 to 15 cm) below heat until browned on top (about 6 minutes). Then turn chops over; top equally with mustard mixture, then bread crumbs. Continue to broil until meat is done medium-rare; cut to test (about 6 more minutes).

Arrange potatoes on a platter; arrange chops atop potatoes. Garnish with parsley sprigs, if desired.

Makes 4 servings

Prep: *About 15 minutes*
Cook: *About 1 hour*

Per serving: *422 calories, 13 g total fat, 3 g saturated fat, 61 mg cholesterol, 627 mg sodium, 46 g carbohydrates, 4 g fiber, 25 g protein, 37 mg calcium, 3 mg iron*

Cooking tips: *Quick-cooking cuts of lamb include loin chops, arm chops, boneless sirloin roasts (perfect for four servings or for two meals for two), shoulder chops or blade steaks, and sirloin steaks (also labeled lamb steaks or sirloin chops).*

Choose simple accompaniments for this crisp-skinned whole bird: sliced avocados and fresh thyme leaves drizzled with olive oil and balsamic vinegar, hot French bread, and Meringue Cloud with Strawberries (page 92).

Mustard Roast Chicken

1 chicken (about 4 lbs./1.8 kg), giblets removed

5 tablespoons (75 ml) coarse-grained or regular Dijon mustard

1 teaspoon dried thyme

½ teaspoon ground nutmeg

6 tablespoons (90 ml) evaporated skim milk

12 ounces (340 g) mushrooms (caps 1 to 1½ inches/2.5 to 3.5 cm wide)

1 tablespoon butter or margarine

1 tablespoon (15 ml) lemon juice

1½ teaspoons dried or drained canned green peppercorns

About 4 ounces (115 g) watercress, rinsed and crisped

Salt

Pepper

Rinse chicken inside and out and pat dry. Set chicken, breast up, on a V-shaped rack in a 9- by 13-inch baking pan.

In a small bowl, mix 3 tablespoons (45 ml) of the mustard, thyme, and nutmeg. Loosen skin of chicken breast by easing your fingers under it from front and back of bird; leave skin in place. Spread half the mustard mixture over breast meat beneath skin. Add 2 tablespoons (30 ml) of the milk to remaining mustard mixture; set aside.

Roast chicken in a 400°F (205°C) oven for 30 minutes. Spoon remaining mustard mixture over legs and wings, letting it flow into joint crevices. Continue to roast until bird is richly browned and meat near thighbone is no longer pink; cut to test (25 to 30 more minutes).

Meanwhile, cut mushrooms in half through caps; then place in a 10- or 12-inch omelette pan and add butter, lemon juice, and peppercorns. Cook over high heat, stirring often, until liquid has evaporated and mushrooms are lightly browned (4 to 5 minutes). Remove from heat and keep warm.

Tilt chicken to drain juices into baking pan. Transfer chicken to a platter and spoon mushrooms alongside; keep warm. Skim and discard fat from pan drippings. Add remaining ¼ cup (60 ml) milk and remaining 2 tablespoons (30 ml) mustard to drippings. Bring to a rolling boil over high heat, stirring constantly. Tilt chicken platter to spoon juices from platter into sauce. Stir sauce; then pour it into a serving dish. Garnish chicken with watercress. Serve with sauce; season to taste with salt and pepper.

Makes 4 to 6 servings

Prep: *About 15 minutes*
Cook: *About 1 hour*

Per serving: *491 calories, 28 g total fat, 9 g saturated fat, 149 mg cholesterol, 375 mg sodium, 7 g carbohydrates, 2 g fiber, 48 g protein, 118 mg calcium, 4 mg iron*

Chunky with vegetables and cubes of chicken breast, this pot pie is a one-dish meal. For dessert, serve hot coffee, gingersnaps, and a selection of fresh fruit in season. Try sliced peaches and plums; or choose persimmons, pomegranates, and pears.

Chicken Pot Pie

1 *sheet frozen puff pastry (about 8½ oz./245 g)*

1½ *quarts (1.4 liters) fat-free reduced-sodium chicken broth*

4 *boneless, skinless chicken breast halves (about 1½ lbs./680 g total)*

3 *medium-size carrots, diced*

12 *ounces (340 g) red thin-skinned potatoes, scrubbed and diced*

1 *cup (120 g) thinly sliced celery*

1 *cup (240 ml) low-fat milk*

⅓ *cup (40 g) all-purpose flour*

1 *teaspoon ground sage or 2 teaspoons minced fresh sage*

½ *cup (73 g) frozen tiny peas*

Salt

Pepper

1 *egg, lightly beaten*

Sage sprigs (optional)

Place frozen pastry on a clean, dry surface to thaw before unfolding.

In a 3- or 4-quart pan, bring broth to a boil over high heat; boil, uncovered, until reduced to 3 cups/710 ml (about 15 minutes). Meanwhile, rinse chicken, pat dry, and cut into 1-inch (2.5-cm) pieces.

Add chicken, carrots, potatoes, and celery to broth. Return to a boil; boil for 3 minutes (vegetables will still be firm).

In a jar, combine milk, flour, and ground sage; close jar and shake until mixture is smoothly blended. Stirring constantly, pour flour mixture into chicken mixture; bring to a boil, stirring. Reduce heat to a simmer and stir until sauce is thickened (about 1 minute). Stir in peas, then season to taste with salt and pepper. Pour mixture into a 9- by 13-inch baking pan.

Unfold puff pastry and place over filling in baking pan. Brush top of pastry lightly with egg. Bake in a 400°F (205°C) oven until pastry puffs and is a rich, shiny dark gold (10 to 12 minutes). To serve, spoon chicken filling and some of the pastry into wide, shallow soup bowls. Garnish with sage sprigs, if desired.

Makes 6 to 8 servings

Prep: *About 20 minutes*
Cook: *About 40 minutes*

Per serving: *423 calories, 16 g total fat, 3 g saturated fat, 90 mg cholesterol, 704 mg sodium, 36 g carbohydrates, 3 g fiber, 32 g protein, 80 mg calcium, 3 mg iron*

Cooking tips: *For covering pot pies, frozen puff pastry is a quick alternative to homemade pie crust or biscuit dough. This kind of pastry is best eaten warm. If you like, bake biscuits the next day to serve with any leftover pie.*

Serve with hot jasmine or basmati rice and thinly sliced cucumbers doused with seasoned rice vinegar. For sipping, you might try tall glasses of Thai-style iced tea—strong tea with sweetened condensed milk. Cantaloupe wedges with mint make a refreshing conclusion.

Coconut Basil Chicken

2 pounds (905 g) boneless, skinless chicken breasts

2 to 4 tablespoons (30 to 60 ml) salad oil

1 medium-size onion (about 6 oz./170 g), thinly sliced

3 cloves garlic, minced

2 tablespoons minced fresh ginger

1 or 2 fresh jalapeño chiles, seeded and slivered

¾ cup (180 ml) low-fat coconut milk

¼ cup (60 ml) soy sauce

3 tablespoons (45 ml) rice vinegar or 2 tablespoons (30 ml) distilled white vinegar

1½ cups (60 g) lightly packed slivered fresh basil

Basil sprigs

1 small fresh hot red chile (optional)

Slivered green bell pepper (optional)

Hot cooked rice

Rinse chicken, pat dry, and cut crosswise into strips about ¼ inch (6 mm) wide. Set aside.

Preheat a 14-inch wok or 12-inch omelette pan over high heat until rim of pan is hot-to-the-touch. Add 2 tablespoons (30 ml) of the oil and wait for about 1 more minute. Add onion, garlic, ginger, and slivered jalapeño chiles; cook, stirring often, until onion is light golden (about 2 minutes). Spoon onion mixture into a bowl and set aside.

Add chicken strips to pan, about a third at a time; cook, stirring occasionally, until tinged with brown (about 3 minutes). As chicken is cooked, remove it from pan and set aside with onion mixture. If needed, add more oil to pan to prevent sticking.

When all chicken has been cooked, pour coconut milk, soy sauce, and vinegar into pan. Bring to a boil; then boil, uncovered, until reduced by a third (about 5 minutes). Return onion mixture and chicken to pan; stir to coat with sauce. Add slivered basil; stir to heat through. Garnish with basil sprigs and, if desired, whole red chile and bell pepper slivers. Serve over rice.

Makes 6 servings

Prep: About 15 minutes
Cook: About 20 minutes

Per serving: 302 calories, 10 g total fat, 2 g saturated fat, 88 mg cholesterol, 799 mg sodium, 12 g carbohydrates, 1 g fiber, 37 g protein, 218 mg calcium, 5 mg iron

Cooking tips: If you don't have fresh chiles, season the dish to taste with ground red pepper (cayenne), liquid hot pepper seasoning, crushed red pepper flakes, or hot chile oil. All of these will keep at room temperature on your kitchen shelf. Add them along with the liquid in the recipe.

This Cajun-Creole dish traditionally includes sausage, ham, and shellfish or poultry, but the following simplified version features just one kind of meat—lean turkey sausage. For a family meal, add a green salad and a pitcher of iced tea. End with peach sorbet topped with raspberries.

A Leaner Jambalaya

1 tablespoon (15 ml) salad oil

1 large onion (about 8 oz./230 g), chopped

1 large green bell pepper (about 8 oz./230 g), seeded and cut into thin strips

1 cup (120 g) thinly sliced celery

4 cloves garlic, minced or pressed

2 or 3 fresh jalapeño chiles, seeded and minced

2 pounds (905 g) hot turkey Italian sausage, casings removed, meat cut into 1-inch (2.5-cm) pieces

2 cups (370 g) long-grain white rice

2 cans (about 14½ oz./415 g each) tomatoes

1 quart (950 ml) fat-free reduced-sodium chicken broth

4 green onions, thinly sliced

½ cup (20 g) chopped parsley

Celery leaves and parsley sprigs (optional)

Salt

Pepper

Preheat a 10- or 12-inch omelette pan over medium-high heat until rim of pan is hot-to-the-touch. Add oil and wait for about 1 more minute. Add chopped onion and cook, stirring often, until translucent around edges (about 5 minutes). Add bell pepper, celery, garlic, chiles, and sausage. Continue to cook, stirring often, until onion is soft (about 10 more minutes).

Mix rice into vegetables and sausage; stir until grains brown slightly (1 to 2 minutes). Add tomatoes (break up with a spoon) and their liquid, then broth; bring to a boil, stirring occasionally. Then reduce heat, cover, and simmer until liquid has been absorbed and rice is tender to bite (20 to 30 minutes). Stir in green onions and chopped parsley. Spoon onto a platter or plates; garnish with celery leaves and parsley sprigs, if desired. Season to taste with salt and pepper.

Makes 8 servings

Prep: *About 25 minutes*
Cook: *About 45 minutes*

Per serving: *428 calories, 15 g total fat, 4 g saturated fat, 61 mg cholesterol, 1,211 mg sodium, 50 g carbohydrates, 3 g fiber, 26 g protein, 94 mg calcium, 6 mg iron*

Cooking tips: *A French knife has a triangular shape, a design that makes it easy to rock the knife back and forth for speedy chopping and slicing. One hand holds the knife tip in place; the other quickly moves the handle up and down.*

Serve this lean, spicy-sweet dish with plain white rice, black beans, and ginger beer or iced herbal tea. For a dessert in keeping with the Caribbean theme, choose Key lime pie or bowls of sliced bananas with sweetened sour cream and coconut.

Turkey Picadillo

1   *tablespoon (15 ml) olive oil*

1   *large onion (about 8 oz./230 g), diced*

1   *large red bell pepper (about 8 oz./230 g), seeded and chopped*

2   *cloves garlic, minced*

1   *small fresh jalapeño chile, seeded and minced*

1   *pound ground turkey*

1   *can (about 14½ oz./415 g) diced tomatoes*

¾   *cup (180 ml) fat-free reduced-sodium chicken broth*

½   *cup (70 g) golden raisins*

¼   *cup (35 g) pimento-stuffed green olives, sliced*

2   *tablespoons drained capers*

1   *dried bay leaf (optional)*

½   *teaspoon ground cumin*

1   *small fresh hot green chile (optional)*

Lime wedges

Salt

Pepper

Preheat a 3- or 5-quart sauté pan or 10- or 12-inch omelette pan over medium-high heat until rim of pan is hot-to-the-touch. Add oil and wait for about 1 more minute. Add onion, bell pepper, garlic, and minced jalapeño chile; cook, stirring often, until onion begins to soften (about 8 minutes).

Add turkey and cook until lightly browned (about 8 minutes), stirring with a wide spatula to break up meat. Add tomatoes, broth, raisins, olives, capers, bay leaf (if desired), and cumin. Bring to a boil; then reduce heat, cover, and simmer until flavors are blended (about 30 minutes). Garnish with whole chile (if desired) and lime. Season to taste with salt and pepper.

Makes 4 servings

Prep: *About 20 minutes*
Cook: *About 45 minutes*

Per serving: *317 calories, 13 g total fat, 3 g saturated fat, 83 mg cholesterol, 699 mg sodium, 28 g carbohydrates, 4 g fiber, 23 g protein, 77 mg calcium, 3 mg iron*

Cooking tips: *Using canned diced tomatoes instead of fresh ones saves you the trouble of coring and chopping. If you prefer to substitute fresh tomatoes in a recipe calling for the canned variety, use 2 or 3 medium-size tomatoes, chopped, for each 14½-ounce (415-g) can.*

Serve sliced papayas and avocados alongside these fajitas; offer lime or lemon wedges to season both fajitas and fruit. Alongside, serve a vinaigrette-dressed salad of canned black and white beans with cilantro, bacon, and minced onion. For dessert, offer a flan or ice cream.

Stove-top Turkey Fajitas

¼ cup (60 ml) lime juice

1 tablespoon (15 ml) balsamic or red wine vinegar

1 clove garlic, minced or pressed

½ teaspoon honey

¼ teaspoon ground coriander

2 teaspoons ground cumin

1 pound (455 g) turkey breast tenderloins

1 large green bell pepper (about 8 oz./230 g)

1 medium-size red onion (about 8 oz./230 g)

2 tablespoons (30 ml) salad oil

Salt

4 warm flour tortillas (each about 10 inches/25 cm in diameter)

Lime or lemon wedges

Reduced-fat sour cream (optional)

Purchased salsa (optional)

In a large bowl, mix lime juice, vinegar, garlic, honey, coriander, and cumin. Rinse turkey and pat dry; then cut each tenderloin crosswise into slices about ⅛ inch (3 mm) thick. Stir turkey into marinade and let stand for about 10 minutes, stirring several times. Meanwhile, seed and thinly slice bell pepper; thinly slice onion.

Drain turkey and discard marinade. Set turkey aside. Preheat a 10- or 12-inch omelette pan over high heat until rim of pan is hot-to-the-touch. Add 1 tablespoon (15 ml) of the oil and wait for about 1 more minute. Add bell pepper and onion; cook, stirring, until pepper is limp and onion begins to brown (about 3 minutes). Remove from pan and set aside in a serving bowl.

Heat remaining 1 tablespoon (15 ml) oil in pan. Add turkey and cook, stirring often, until no longer pink in center; cut to test (about 3 minutes). Transfer turkey to bowl with vegetables. Season to taste with salt.

To serve, divide turkey and vegetables among tortillas. Season to taste with lime; top with sour cream and salsa, if desired. Roll to enclose and eat out of hand.

Makes 4 servings

Prep: *About 5 minutes, plus 10 minutes to marinate*
Cook: *About 6 minutes*

Per serving: *406 calories, 12 g total fat, 2 g saturated fat, 70 mg cholesterol, 328 mg sodium, 40 g carbohydrates, 3 g fiber, 34 g protein, 107 mg calcium, 4 mg iron*

Cooking tips: *For a faster meal, buy cooked marinated turkey breast at the grocery store or deli. Cut it into thin strips; then serve it in warm flour tortillas along with red onion rings, sliced green bell pepper, and avocado slices.*

Crisp-crusted salmon fillets served with juicy fresh grapefruit segments and a tart grapefruit mayonnaise make an elegant entrée. Complete the menu with a watercress and nasturtium salad, Coconut Rice (page 40), and scoops of lemon sorbet-sprinkled with shredded mint.

Crusted Salmon with Grapefruit & Grapefruit Mayonnaise

1   cup (240 ml) grapefruit
    juice

¾   cup (180 ml) reduced-fat or
    regular mayonnaise

3   tablespoons drained capers

2   tablespoons chopped
    fresh mint or ½ teaspoon
    dried mint

6   slices (about 7½ oz./215 g)
    firm-textured white bread
    (crusts removed), processed
    in a food processor to make
    coarse, even crumbs

3   large grapefruit (about
    1 lb./455 g each)

2   large egg whites

    About 2⅓ pounds (1.1 kg)
    boneless, skinless salmon
    fillet (about 1 inch/2.5 cm
    thick), cut into 6 equal
    pieces

2   tablespoons butter or
    margarine

    Mint sprigs

Pour grapefruit juice into an 8- or 10-inch omelette pan. Bring to a boil over high heat; then boil, uncovered, until reduced to ¼ cup/60 ml (about 5 minutes). Pour juice into a bowl; refrigerate until cool. In another bowl, mix mayonnaise, capers, and chopped mint; stir in cooled juice, then cover and refrigerate.

Spread bread crumbs in an 8- or 9-inch-square cake pan; bake in a 325°F (160°C) oven, stirring often, until crisp but not browned (10 to 15 minutes). Let cool slightly.

Meanwhile, cut off and discard peel and all white membrane from grapefruit. Holding fruit over a bowl, cut between membranes to release segments; drop segments into bowl, discarding any seeds. Set aside.

In a wide, shallow bowl, beat egg whites to blend. Pour crumbs into another wide, shallow bowl. Rinse fish and pat dry. Roll pieces of fish, one at a time, in egg whites; drain briefly, then coat with crumbs. Set pieces slightly apart on a sheet of wax paper.

Preheat a 10- or 12-inch omelette pan over medium heat until rim of pan is hot-to-the-touch. Add 1 tablespoon of the butter and wait for about 1 more minute. Add fish, a portion at a time (do not crowd pan). Cook, turning once, until browned on both sides (about 5 minutes). As fish is browned, transfer it to a 9- by 13-inch baking pan; add remaining butter to omelette pan as needed to prevent sticking. When all fish has been browned, place baking pan in a 325°F (165°C) oven. Bake until fish is just opaque but still moist in thickest part; cut to test (5 to 8 minutes).

Lift grapefruit from bowl and arrange on 6 individual plates. Set one piece of fish on each plate. Garnish with mint sprigs; accompany with grapefruit mayonnaise.

Makes 6 servings

Prep: *35 minutes*
Cook: *About 35 minutes*

Per serving: *457 calories, 16 g total fat, 4 g saturated fat, 108 mg cholesterol, 646 mg sodium, 35 g carbohydrates, 1 g fiber, 40 g protein, 78 mg calcium, 3 mg iron*

Delicate sole fillets in a lemony sauce are delicious with rice and fresh green beans topped with sliced almonds. For dessert, serve orange or tangerine sorbet and crunchy chocolate biscotti.

Fillet of Sole with Shallots, Vermouth & Thyme

1½   *pounds (680 g) fillet of sole*

2   *to 4 tablespoons all-purpose flour*

  About 1 tablespoon butter or margarine

  About 1 tablespoon (15 ml) salad oil

¾   *cup (120 g) finely chopped shallots*

½   *cup (120 ml) dry vermouth*

½   *cup (120 ml) fat-free reduced-sodium chicken broth*

1   *tablespoon (15 ml) lemon juice*

1   *teaspoon minced fresh thyme or ¼ teaspoon dried thyme*

  Thyme sprigs

  Lemon wedges

  Salt

Rinse fish and pat dry. Coat each piece with flour and shake off excess; then arrange fish on a sheet of wax paper, keeping pieces in a single layer.

Preheat a 3- or 5-quart sauté pan over medium-high heat until rim of pan is hot-to-the-touch. Add 1 teaspoon each of the butter and oil; wait for about 1 more minute. Then add fish pieces, a portion at a time (do not crowd pan). Cook, turning once, until fish is just opaque but still moist in thickest part; cut to test (3 to 5 minutes). As fish is cooked, transfer it to a platter and keep warm. Add more butter and oil to pan as needed to prevent sticking.

When all fish has been cooked, add shallots to pan. Cook over medium heat, stirring often, until translucent (3 to 5 minutes). Add vermouth, broth, lemon juice, and minced thyme. Increase heat to high and bring to a boil; then boil, uncovered, until sauce is reduced by half (3 to 5 minutes).

Spoon sauce over fish; garnish with thyme sprigs and lemon wedges. Season to taste with salt.

Makes 4 servings

Prep: *About 15 minutes*
Cook: *About 20 minutes*

Per serving: *264 calories, 8 g total fat, 3 g saturated fat, 89 mg cholesterol, 245 mg sodium, 12 g carbohydrates, .34 g fiber, 34 g protein, 48 mg calcium, 1 mg iron*

Cooking tips: *Butter gives superb flavor to sautéed foods, but high or prolonged heat causes it to burn. To enjoy a buttery flavor with no worries about scorching, use a mixture of half butter, half vegetable oil.*

Serve these meaty tuna steaks with squares of hot cornbread and a salad of bell pepper, crisp corn kernels, and cherry tomatoes in a lime vinaigrette dressing. Or, if you like, offer hot cooked rice or black beans in place of the bread.

Ahi Margarita

½ cup (120 ml) tequila

⅓ cup (80 ml) lime juice

1½ tablespoons (23 ml) olive oil

½ teaspoon paprika

1 teaspoon grated orange zest

4 ahi tuna steaks, each about 1¾ inches (4.5 cm) thick (about 1½ lbs./680 g total)

¼ cup (60 ml) nonfat sour cream

Cilantro sprigs (optional)

Salt

In a shallow dish, mix tequila, lime juice, 1 teaspoon of the oil, paprika, and orange zest. Rinse fish and pat dry; place in tequila mixture and turn to coat. Let stand for 5 to 10 minutes, turning a few times.

Remove fish from marinade, reserving marinade. Blot fish dry with paper towels. Preheat a grill pan or omelette pan over medium-high heat until rim of pan is hot-to-the-touch. Add remaining 3½ teaspoons (18 ml) oil and wait for about 1 more minute. Then add fish and cook, turning once, until both sides are lightly browned and edges have turned white ¼ to ⅓ inch (6 to 8 mm) in from top and bottom surfaces (10 to 14 minutes). When fish is done, it will still be rosy in center; cut to test. Remove from pan and keep warm; scrape browned bits free from pan bottom and discard them.

Quickly pour marinade into pan used to cook fish. Bring to a boil over high heat; boil, uncovered, until reduced to about ⅔ cup/160 ml (2 to 4 minutes). Remove from heat and pour into a small bowl; whisk in sour cream. Spoon sauce over fish. Garnish with cilantro sprigs, if desired; season to taste with salt.

Makes 4 servings

Prep: *About 5 minutes, plus 5 to 10 minutes to marinate*
Cook: *About 15 minutes*

Per serving: *294 calories, 7 g total fat, 1 g saturated fat, 68 mg cholesterol, 70 mg sodium, 3 g carbohydrates, 0 g fiber, 37 g protein, 47 mg calcium, 1 mg iron*

Cooking tips: *These small, thick cuts of tuna resemble filet mignon. To be the right size—small, but still thick—they must be cut from the tail end of the tuna.*

Halibut steaks in a vivid, herb-seasoned tomato sauce make a beautifully slim entrée. Keep up the lean and healthful theme with a basket of French rolls and, for dessert, sliced oranges and hot espresso.

Baked Halibut Provençal

1   tablespoon (15 ml) salad oil

2   cups (340 g) diced onions

1   cup (120 g) diced celery

2   cloves garlic, minced or pressed

2   cans (about 14½ oz./ 415 g each) pear-shaped tomatoes, drained

2   tablespoons (30 ml) lime juice

1   cup (240 ml) dry white wine

2   tablespoons herbes de Provence (or about ¾ teaspoon each dried basil, marjoram, oregano, rosemary, savory, thyme, and crushed fennel seeds)

3   pounds (1.35 kg) halibut steaks (each about 1 inch/ 2.5 cm thick), cut into 8 equal pieces

    Tarragon sprigs

    Salt

    Pepper

Preheat an 11- by 14-inch roasting pan over medium-high heat until rim of pan is hot-to-the-touch. Add oil and wait for about 1 more minute. Add onions, celery, and garlic. Cook, stirring, until onions begin to brown at edges (about 7 minutes). Stir in tomatoes (break up with a spoon), lime juice, wine, and herbes de Provence. Remove from heat.

Rinse fish, pat dry, and arrange atop tomato mixture. Bake in a 425°F (230°C) oven until fish is just opaque but still moist in thickest part; cut to test (about 10 minutes).

Arrange fish on a platter or in a shallow bowl; spoon sauce over fish. Garnish with tarragon sprigs. Season to taste with salt and pepper.

Makes 8 servings

Prep: *About 20 minutes*
Cook: *About 20 minutes*

Per serving: *227 calories, 5 g total fat, 1 g saturated fat, 44 mg cholesterol, 258 mg sodium, 9 g carbohydrates, 2 g fiber, 30 g protein, 111 mg calcium, 2 mg iron*

Cooking tips: *If you can't find halibut, you may substitute swordfish, shark, or sea bass.*

This bistro dish is great with sliced fresh tomatoes and a crusty baguette for sopping up the delicious juices. Serve with chardonnay or a flavored sparkling water with crushed ice and citrus slices; for dessert, offer ginger or lemon scones split and filled with ice cream and fruit.

Sautéed Shrimp with Fried Garlic & Green Beans

8 ounces (230 g) slender green beans (ends trimmed)

3 tablespoons (45 ml) olive oil

  Salt

  Pepper

1 pound (455 g) raw shrimp (15 to 20 per lb.), shelled (leave tails on) and deveined

1 tablespoon finely chopped garlic

1 tablespoon (15 ml) sherry vinegar

2 tablespoons chopped parsley

  Dash of ground red pepper (cayenne)

Cut beans in half diagonally; or cut into 2- to 3-inch (5- to 8-cm) lengths. Place beans in an 8-inch-square cake pan. Drizzle with 1 tablespoon (15 ml) of the oil and stir beans to coat; sprinkle with salt and pepper. Cover and bake in a 450°F (230°C) oven until heated through but still tender-crisp to bite (about 15 minutes).

About 3 minutes before beans are done, preheat a 3- or 5-quart sauté pan over high heat until rim of pan is hot-to-the-touch. Add 1 tablespoon (15 ml) of the oil and wait for about 1 more minute. Then add shrimp and cook, stirring often, until just opaque in center; cut to test (2 to 3 minutes).

Divide beans equally among 4 individual plates; arrange shrimp alongside beans. Keep warm.

In sauté pan, combine garlic and remaining 1 tablespoon (15 ml) oil. Cook over medium-high heat, stirring often, until garlic is golden brown (about 1 minute). Add vinegar and stir for about 30 seconds, scraping any browned bits free from pan bottom. Immediately pour mixture over beans and shrimp; sprinkle with parsley and red pepper and serve at once.

Makes 4 servings

Prep: *About 30 minutes*
Cook: *About 20 minutes*

Per serving: *209 calories, 12 g total fat, 2 g saturated fat, 140 mg cholesterol, 141 mg sodium, 6 g carbohydrates, 1 g fiber, 20 g protein, 76 mg calcium, 3 mg iron*

Cooking tips: *To devein shrimp, insert a wooden pick or slender skewer between shell segments and lift out vein. Repeat in several places, if necessary. You can also buy shrimp already shelled and deveined, but expect to pay about twice as much per pound.*

Crisp crab cakes need nothing more than a good coleslaw alongside—perhaps a colorful combination of shredded red and green cabbage, slivered pickled ginger, and chopped bell pepper dressed with seasoned rice vinegar. Offer sesame breadsticks and tall glasses of iced tea.

Crab Cakes with Lime Splash

2　*large eggs*

⅓　*cup (15 g) fine dry bread crumbs*

1　*tablespoon (15 ml) Worcestershire sauce*

½　*teaspoon celery seeds*

¼　*teaspoon dry mustard*

¼　*teaspoon curry powder*

¼　*teaspoon ground red pepper (cayenne)*

⅛　*teaspoon ground cloves*

1　*pound (455 g) cooked crabmeat*

1　*tablespoon butter or margarine*

¼　*cup (60 ml) lime juice*

1　*teaspoon minced fresh jalapeño chile*

In a large bowl, beat eggs to blend. Add bread crumbs, Worcestershire sauce, celery seeds, mustard, curry powder, red pepper, and cloves; mix well. Add crabmeat and mix gently, being careful not to break up lumps of crab. Shape crab mixture into 8 equal patties.

Preheat a 10- or 12-inch omelette pan over medium heat until rim of pan is hot-to-the-touch. Add butter and wait for about 1 more minute. Then add crab patties and cook, turning once, until golden brown on both sides (about 10 minutes).

Meanwhile, in a small bowl, mix lime juice and chile; set aside.

To serve, arrange 2 crab cakes on each plate; offer lime juice mixture to spoon over crab cakes.

Makes 4 servings

Prep: *About 10 minutes*
Cook: *About 10 minutes*

Per serving: *223 calories, 8 g total fat, 3 g saturated fat, 228 mg cholesterol, 499 mg sodium, 9 g carbohydrates, .42 g fiber, 27 g protein, 160 mg calcium, 2 mg iron*

Cooking tips: *Before using crab, carefully pick through it to remove any pieces of shell. To reduce fat, try seasoning fried fish dishes with lemon, lime, or vinegar (spiked with chiles, garlic, ginger, or just salt) instead of mayonnaise-based sauces.*

Here's a lovely way to serve a springtime favorite. Slender fresh asparagus spears are cooked just until tender, then topped with a light orange sauce and a sprinkling of toasted almonds and prosciutto. The dish is delicious with grilled tenderloin steaks and boiled new potatoes.

Prosciutto-Almond Asparagus

1 tablespoon (15 ml) olive oil

2 ounces (55 g) paper-thin slices prosciutto, cut crosswise into strips about ⅓ inch (5 mm) wide

⅓ cup (40 g) sliced almonds

¾ cup (180 ml) fresh orange juice

3 tablespoons (45 ml) red wine vinegar

1 teaspoon cornstarch

1 teaspoon grated orange zest

2 pounds (905 g) asparagus, tough ends snapped off

Twist of orange zest

Salt

Pepper

Preheat a 10- or 12-inch omelette pan over medium heat until rim of pan is hot-to-the-touch. Add oil and wait for about 1 more minute. Then add prosciutto and cook, stirring often, until browned (about 4 minutes). With a slotted spoon, remove prosciutto from pan; drain on paper towels.

Add almonds to pan and stir until golden (2 to 3 minutes). With slotted spoon, remove almonds from pan; drain on paper towels. Discard oil in pan.

In a small bowl, mix orange juice, vinegar, cornstarch, and grated orange zest until smooth. Pour into pan; increase heat to high and cook, stirring, until sauce is bubbly (about 1 minute). Pour into a small serving bowl; keep hot.

Rinse pan. Place asparagus in pan and add ½ cup (120 ml) water. Cover and bring to a boil over high heat; then reduce heat and simmer until asparagus is tender-crisp to bite (about 7 minutes), stirring halfway through cooking. Drain and arrange on a platter.

Pour orange sauce over asparagus; top with prosciutto and almonds. Garnish with a twist of orange zest; season to taste with salt and pepper.

Makes 6 servings

Prep: *About 10 minutes*
Cook: *About 20 minutes*

Per serving: *109 calories, 6 g total fat, 1 g saturated fat, 8 mg cholesterol, 178 mg sodium, 9 g carbohydrates, 2 g fiber, 8 g protein, 44 mg calcium, 1 mg iron*

Cooking tips: *Freshly ground pepper is more aromatic and has a sharper, livelier flavor than pepper purchased already ground.*

Foods roasted at high temperatures have a marvelous smoky, almost barbecue-like quality, as you'll discover when you try this medley of roasted winter vegetables. Try them with steak or smoked pork chops; offer baked apples and ice cream for dessert.

Roasted Winter Vegetables

2 tablespoons (30 ml) olive oil

1 pound Yukon gold or russet potatoes, scrubbed and cut into ³/₄-inch (2-cm) cubes

³/₄ cup (about 4 oz./115 g) baby carrots

1 large red onion (about 12 oz./340 g), coarsely chopped

1 medium-size yam or sweet potato (about 8 oz./230 g)

1 large beet (about 8 oz./230 g)

Minced Italian parsley and Italian parsley sprigs

Salt

Pepper

Pour oil into a 9- by 13-inch au gratin pan or 11- by 14-inch roasting pan. Place pan in a 500°F (260°C) oven and heat just until oil is hot (about 1¹/₂ minutes). Stir in Yukon gold potatoes, carrots, and red onion. Cook for 15 minutes, stirring after 10 minutes.

Meanwhile, peel yam and beet; cut each into about ¹/₂-inch (1-cm) cubes.

Add yam and beet to pan; continue to cook until vegetables are golden brown and yam mashes easily when pressed (about 20 more minutes), stirring every 10 minutes.

Serve vegetables from pan or spoon them onto a platter. Garnish with parsley; season to taste with salt and pepper.

Makes 4 servings

Prep: *About 10 minutes*
Cook: *About 35 minutes*

Per serving: *273 calories, 7 g total fat, 1 g saturated fat, 0 mg cholesterol, 61 mg sodium, 49 g carbohydrates, 6 g fiber, 5 g protein, 47 mg calcium, 2 mg iron*

Cooking tips: *Use the same high-temperature technique to roast asparagus spears for 5 to 7 minutes; then douse them with balsamic vinegar and serve with broiled fish or barbecued chicken.*

This French-style pizza has a thin, crisp crust, a robust tomato-herb sauce, and a topping of nutty-tasting Niçoise olives. The cheese? Just a sprinkling. Serve the pizza with soup for lunch; or offer it as a side dish for lamb chops, a steak, or roasted chicken.

Provençal Pizza

1¾ cups (201 g) thinly slivered onions

3 large cloves garlic, thinly sliced

1 teaspoon olive oil

1 cup (240 ml) water

1 can (about 6 oz./170 g) unsalted tomato paste

1½ teaspoons herbes de Provence (or ¼ teaspoon each dried basil, marjoram, oregano, rosemary, savory, thyme, and crushed fennel seeds)

1 loaf (about 1 lb./455 g) frozen bread dough, thawed

⅔ cup (55 g) shredded Parmesan cheese

1 ounce (28 g) canned anchovies, drained, patted dry, and halved lengthwise (optional)

¼ cup (28 g) Niçoise or pitted ripe olives

In a 10- or 12-inch omelette pan, combine onions, garlic, oil, and ¼ cup (60 ml) of the water. Cover and cook over medium-low heat until water has evaporated (10 to 12 minutes). Stir in ¼ cup (60 ml) more water; cover and continue to cook, stirring occasionally, until water has evaporated and onions are very soft and golden (15 to 20 more minutes).

In a small bowl, mix tomato paste, herbes de Provence, and remaining ½ cup (120 ml) water.

On a floured board, knead dough briefly to expel air. Gather dough into a smooth ball; then roll out to a 14-inch (35.5-cm) circle. Drape dough over rolling pin; transfer to a floured 14-inch pizza pan.

Spread dough with tomato paste mixture; top evenly with onion mixture, then cheese. If using anchovies, crisscross pairs of anchovy pieces to form evenly spaced "X" shapes over pizza. Distribute olives evenly over pizza; press into dough.

Bake pizza in a 500°F (260°C) oven until crust is browned and crisp (9 to 12 minutes). To serve, cut pizza into wedges; if you used Niçoise olives, watch out for pits as you eat.

Makes 6 to 8 servings

Prep: *About 10 minutes*
Cook: *About 45 minutes*

Per serving: *259 calories, 7 g total fat, 2 g saturated fat, 9 mg cholesterol, 515 mg sodium, 40 g carbohydrates, 2 g fiber, 10 g protein, 156 mg calcium, 2 mg iron*

Cooking tips: *Other cooked vegetables make good pizza toppings, too; try sliced zucchini, spinach, diced potato, or corn kernels.*

A helping of these fluffy, creamy potatoes and a few spears of lemon-buttered broccoli are perfect partners for broiled salmon steaks or a juicy beef roast. To complete a home-style menu, serve mud balls: chocolate ice cream rolled in chopped chocolate and presented on a pool of fudge sauce.

Garlic Mashed Potatoes

1   *head garlic*

4   *pounds (1.8 kg) medium-size red thin-skinned potatoes, scrubbed*

1½   *cups (360 ml) hot nonfat milk, whole milk, or whipping cream*

¼   *cup (10 g) minced mixed fresh herbs, such as rosemary, thyme, sage, chives, parsley, or tarragon (use at least 4 kinds), optional*

Butter or margarine (optional)

Salt

Pepper

Place garlic in a small baking pan or dish. Roast in a 400°F (205°C) oven until skin is brown and sides give easily when squeezed (about 40 minutes). Let cool.

While garlic is roasting, place unpeeled potatoes in a 6- or 8-quart pan; add water to cover. Cover pan and bring water to a boil over high heat; then reduce heat and simmer, covered, until potatoes are tender throughout when pierced (about 25 minutes). Drain. If desired, let potatoes stand until cool enough to handle; then peel. Return potatoes to cooking pan and add milk.

With your fingers, pull garlic cloves from head. Pinch each clove to squeeze garlic from skin; add garlic to potatoes. Then add herbs to potatoes, if desired.

With a potato masher, mash potatoes until they are as smooth or chunky as you like. Season to taste with butter (if desired), salt, and pepper.

Makes 8 servings

Prep: *About 20 minutes*
Cook: *About 40 minutes*

Per serving: *213 calories, 1 g total fat, .05 g saturated fat, 1 mg cholesterol, 43 mg sodium, 46 g carbohydrates, 4 g fiber, 6 g protein, 73 mg calcium, 2 mg iron*

Cooking tips: *If you make your mashed potatoes from unpeeled potatoes, they'll be more healthful—and what's more, you'll both save time and give the dish a rustic look. When you choose garlic to roast for this recipe, remember that large cloves are easier to peel than small ones.*

These crusty country-style potatoes are just right with roasted chicken, grilled meats, or even softly scrambled eggs. Add asparagus spears or a watercress salad alongside; try Apple-Blueberry Crisp (page 88) for dessert.

Red & Sweet Potatoes with Caramelized Onions

3   to 4 tablespoons butter or margarine

2   medium-size red onions (about 1 lb./455 g total), cut into wedges about 1 inch (2.5 cm) wide

1   pound (455 g) medium-size red thin-skinned potatoes, scrubbed

1   pound (455 g) medium-size yams or sweet potatoes

½   teaspoon ground marjoram (optional)

½   teaspoon dried thyme (optional)

½   teaspoon dried rosemary (optional)

   Salt

   Pepper

Preheat a 3- or 5-quart sauté pan or 10- or 12-inch omelette pan over medium-low heat until rim of pan is hot-to-the-touch. Add 1 tablespoon of the butter and wait for about 1 more minute. Add onions and cook, stirring occasionally, until they begin to caramelize (about 40 minutes); onions will become very soft, then look brown-red. Remove onions from pan and set aside.

While onions are cooking, quarter thin-skinned potatoes. Peel yams; as you peel them, drop them in a bowl of cold water to prevent darkening. When all have been peeled, cut them into pieces about the same size as the potato quarters.

Place thin-skinned potatoes and yams in a 3- or 4-quart pan, preferably one with a pasta insert. Add water to cover. Cover pan and bring water to a boil over high heat; then reduce heat and simmer, covered, until potatoes and yams are almost tender when pierced (about 20 minutes). Lift pasta insert to drain potatoes and yams; or pour off water to drain.

In pan used to cook onions, melt 2 more tablespoons butter over medium-high heat. Add potatoes, yams, and, if desired, marjoram, thyme, and rosemary. Cook, stirring occasionally with a wide spatula, until potatoes and yams are lightly browned (15 to 20 minutes); if needed for browning, add an additional 1 tablespoon butter. Stir onions into potato mixture. Season to taste with salt and pepper.

Makes 6 servings

Prep: *About 15 minutes*
Cook: *About 1 hour*

Per serving: *236 calories, 8 g total fat, 5 g saturated fat, 21 mg cholesterol, 98 mg sodium, 39 g carbohydrates, 5 g fiber, 4 g protein, 35 mg calcium, 1 mg iron*

Cooking tips: *Slow-cooking onions in butter or oil over low heat brings out their natural sugars and emphasizes their sweetness. After long cooking, the sugar in the vegetables actually begins to caramelize.*

Serve with a pitcher of cold thick cream or with scoops of vanilla ice cream.

Apple-Blueberry Crisp

4   medium-size tart apples such as Granny Smith or Pippin (about 2 lbs./905 g total)

1   cup (145 g) fresh or frozen blueberries

1   tablespoon all-purpose flour

¼   cup (50 g) granulated sugar

½   teaspoon ground cinnamon

⅓   cup (30 g) rolled oats

¼   cup (30 g) all-purpose flour

¼   cup (55 g) firmly packed brown sugar

¼   cup (30 g) chopped pecans (optional)

2   tablespoons butter or margarine, melted

Peel and core apples; then cut lengthwise into wedges about ¼ inch (6 mm) thick. In a 10-inch paella pan or 2½-quart casserole, mix apples, blueberries, the 1 tablespoon flour, granulated sugar, and cinnamon.

In a small bowl, mix oats, the ¼ cup (30 g) flour, brown sugar, pecans (if desired), and butter until mixture is crumbly. Sprinkle topping evenly over fruit and bake in a 400°F (205°C) oven until topping is nicely browned and apples are tender when pierced (about 30 minutes). Serve warm or cool.

Makes 4 to 6 servings

Prep: *About 20 minutes*
Cook: *About 30 minutes*

Per serving: *274 calories, 6 g total fat, 3 g saturated fat, 12 mg cholesterol, 53 mg sodium, 57 g carbohydrates, 4 g fiber, 2 g protein, 25 mg calcium, 1 mg iron*

Cooking tips: *If you like, substitute blackberries or raspberries for the blueberries in this recipe; or try a combination of all three. Don't use strawberries; they'll lose their bright color.*

Offer this rich, velvety cake and the spiced fruit that tops it with softly whipped cream and black coffee or tea. If you don't have time to prepare both cake and fruit, choose one or the other; either makes a delicious dessert all on its own.

Almond Cake with Stewed Fruit

3   *large eggs, separated*

1½ *cups (300 g) sugar*

¾   *cup (6 oz./170 g) butter or margarine, at room temperature*

½   *cup (120 ml) sour cream*

2   *teaspoons almond extract*

1½ *cups (190 g) all-purpose flour*

¼   *teaspoon baking soda*

¼   *cup (30 g) slivered or sliced almonds (optional)*

1½ *cups (360 ml) white grape juice*

1   *cup (140 g) dried apricots*

1   *cup (140 g) dried figs, halved*

¾   *cup (100 g) dried cherries*

1   *cinnamon stick (about 3 inches/8 cm long)*

5   *whole cloves*

1   *teaspoon grated orange zest*

¼   *vanilla bean, split open lengthwise (or ½ teaspoon vanilla extract)*

2   *medium-size ripe pears such as Bartlett, Comice, or Anjou (about 1 lb./455 g total)*

    Softly whipped cream (optional)

In a large bowl, beat egg whites with an electric mixer on high speed until frothy. Gradually add ¾ cup (150 g) of the sugar, 1 tablespoon at a time; continue to beat, scraping bowl occasionally, until whites hold stiff, moist peaks.

In another large bowl, beat remaining ¾ cup (150 g) sugar, butter, egg yolks, sour cream, and almond extract until smooth. Stir in flour and baking soda until smooth. Pour flour mixture over egg whites; carefully fold it into whites with a rubber spatula.

Pour batter into a greased, floured 9-inch-round cake pan; sprinkle with almonds, if desired. Bake on center rack of a 325°F (165°C) oven until a wooden pick inserted in center of cake comes out clean (50 to 55 minutes). Let cool in pan on a rack for 10 minutes; then turn out onto rack. Let cool slightly or completely before serving.

While cake is baking, prepare stewed fruit. In a 3- or 4-quart pan, combine grape juice, apricots, figs, cherries, cinnamon stick, cloves, and orange zest; also add vanilla bean, if using. Bring to a boil over high heat; then reduce heat, cover, and simmer for 15 minutes. Peel, core, and slice pears; stir into fruit mixture. Cover and continue to simmer until dried fruit is soft and pears are translucent (about 15 more minutes). If using vanilla extract, stir in now. Remove from heat.

To serve, cut cake into wedges. Top each wedge with stewed fruit and softly whipped cream, if desired.

Makes 8 servings

Prep: *About 20 minutes*
Cook: *50 to 55 minutes*

Per serving: *654 calories, 23 g total fat, 13 g saturated fat, 133 mg cholesterol, 255 mg sodium, 109 g carbohydrates, 5 g fiber, 7 g protein, 85 mg calcium, 3 mg iron*

Accompany this fruit dessert with strong coffee or cups of cinnamon-and-cardamom-spiced tea. Another time, you might use blackberries, raspberries, or blueberries in place of the strawberries.

Meringue Cloud with Strawberries

2   *tablespoons pine nuts or slivered almonds*

6   *cups (738 g) strawberries, hulled and halved*

¼   *cup (60 ml) orange-flavored liqueur or orange juice*

About ½ cup (100 g) granulated sugar

3   *large egg whites*

¼   *teaspoon cream of tartar*

1   *tablespoon powdered sugar*

Spread pine nuts in an 8- or 9-inch-round cake pan. Bake in a 350°F (175°C) oven until golden (about 10 minutes). Remove nuts from oven; increase oven temperature to 500°F (260°C).

While pine nuts are toasting, place strawberries in a large bowl and mix with liqueur and 1 to 2 tablespoons granulated sugar (or to taste). Pour into a 10-inch paella pan or a shallow 2-quart oval casserole.

In a large bowl, combine egg whites and cream of tartar; beat with an electric mixer on high speed until foamy. Gradually add 6 tablespoons of the granulated sugar; continue to beat just until whites hold stiff, moist peaks. Mound meringue over center of strawberries. Sprinkle with pine nuts. Sift powdered sugar over meringue.

Bake just until meringue is golden (about 4 minutes). Serve at once.

Makes 6 servings

Prep: *About 10 minutes*
Cook: *About 15 minutes*

Per serving: *167 calories, 2 g total fat, .26 g saturated fat, 0 mg cholesterol, 29 mg sodium, 32 g carbohydrates, 4 g fiber, 3 g protein, 23 mg calcium, 1 mg iron*

Cooking tips: *Strawberries absorb water easily and become mushy in spots. To prevent this problem, wait to rinse and hull the berries until just before using.*

This old favorite is exceptionally quick to make—the ingredients are all poured directly into the baking pan and stirred together right there, saving you the task of washing a mixing bowl. Serve the moist, chocolaty cake with café au lait or a latte.

Quick Chocolate Cake

1½ cups (190 g) all-purpose flour

1 cup (200 g) granulated sugar

3 tablespoons unsweetened cocoa

1 teaspoon baking soda

½ teaspoon salt

⅓ cup (80 ml) salad oil

1 tablespoon (15 ml) distilled white vinegar

1 teaspoon vanilla

1 cup (240 ml) cold water

Powdered sugar

In an ungreased 8-inch-square cake pan, mix flour, granulated sugar, cocoa, baking soda, and salt. Make 3 depressions in flour mixture. Pour oil evenly into the 3 depressions; then pour in vinegar and vanilla. Pour water over all; then, using a slotted spatula, mix ingredients thoroughly to form a batter.

Bake in a 350°F (175°C) oven until a wooden pick inserted in center of cake comes out clean (about 35 minutes). Let cool in pan on a rack. Sift powdered sugar over cake before serving.

Makes 9 servings

Prep: *About 10 minutes*
Cook: *About 35 minutes*

Per serving: *242 calories, 8 g total fat, 1 g saturated fat, 0 mg cholesterol, 263 mg sodium, 40 g carbohydrates, 1 g fiber, 3 g protein, 6 mg calcium, 1 mg iron*

Cooking tips: *To make a decorative powdered-sugar pattern on your cake, place a paper doily or solid shape (even a square turned at an angle, or several squares to make a checkerboard) on top of cake. Then rub powdered sugar through a sieve over cake and paper. Gently remove paper, taking care not to spill the sugar. To cut the cake and remove it from the pan, use a coated or nylon spatula; repeated use of metal utensils will damage the pan's surface.*

Index